Copyright © 2023 by Natalie G. Turner (Author)

Thank you for selecting this book as a valuable source of knowledge and inspiration. Our aim is to provide you with insights and information that will enrich your understanding and enhance your personal growth. We appreciate your decision to embark on this journey of discovery with us, and we hope that this book will exceed your expectations and leave a lasting impact on your life.

Title: Perpetual Struggle: The Holy Land Turmoil

Subtitle: The Deep-rooted Strife and Its Uncertain Future in the Middle East

Author: Natalie G. Turner

Table of Contents

Introduce the Israeli-Palestinian conflict and its historical significance.

The Israeli-Palestinian conflict stands as one of the most enduring and deeply rooted disputes in modern history, shaping the landscape of the Middle East for decades. To comprehend the present challenges and the elusive pursuit of peace, it is imperative to journey through the historical intricacies that underpin this protracted struggle.

In the earliest annals of history, the region now known as Israel and Palestine bore witness to the coexistence of diverse cultures and shared heritage. However, the course of time saw the emergence of geopolitical changes, setting the stage for a conflict that would come to define the identity and destiny of the land.

The imposition of the British Mandate in the aftermath of World War I marked a pivotal turning point, setting in motion a series of events that would reverberate for generations. As the mandate evolved, so too did tensions between Jewish and Arab communities, culminating in the birth of the State of Israel in 1948. This seismic event, however, was accompanied by the Nakba, a catastrophic displacement of Palestinians, laying the foundation for animosities that persist to this day.

The Six-Day War of 1967 became a watershed moment, resulting in Israel's occupation of the West Bank, East Jerusalem, and the Gaza Strip. This occupation, fraught with geopolitical significance and territorial disputes, has been a central catalyst for the ongoing conflict.

As we embark on this exploration, it becomes evident that the Israeli-Palestinian conflict is not confined to a mere territorial dispute; it encapsulates the narratives of two peoples deeply connected to the same land, each asserting their historical claims and national aspirations. This introduction serves as an invitation to unravel the layers of history, politics, and identity that converge in the Holy Land, providing a foundational understanding for the chapters that follow.

As we embark on this exploration of the Israeli-Palestinian conflict, it is essential to illuminate the purpose and structure that will guide our journey through the complexities of this enduring struggle. This book seeks to provide a comprehensive understanding of the historical roots, pivotal events, and ongoing challenges that define the Holy Land turmoil.

Purpose of the Book:

At its core, "Perpetual Struggle: The Holy Land Turmoil" aims to shed light on the multifaceted layers of the Israeli-Palestinian conflict. This is not merely a historical account but a nuanced examination that delves into the sociopolitical, cultural, and human dimensions of the conflict. By weaving together narratives from both sides, we strive for a balanced portrayal, acknowledging the diverse perspectives that have shaped the region.

Our purpose extends beyond recounting events; it is a call to comprehend the profound impact of this conflict on the lives of those directly involved and the broader implications for the Middle East. Through this exploration, we hope to foster empathy, understanding, and, ultimately, contribute to the ongoing dialogue for peace.

Structure of the Book:

The structure of "Perpetual Struggle" is designed to provide a chronological and thematic exploration of the conflict. Each chapter serves as a building block, contributing to a comprehensive narrative that unfolds over time. Let's briefly glimpse into the chapters that will guide our journey:

- Chapter 1: Historical Roots of the Conflict: Unveil the ancient history and shared heritage, examining critical events such as the British Mandate, Nakba, and the Six-Day War.

- Chapter 2: Early Peace Initiatives: Explore the United Nations resolutions, the Suez Crisis, Camp David Accords, and the nascent stages of Palestinian Liberation Movements.

- Chapter 3: Oslo Accords and the Peace Process: Examine the Oslo Accords, the role of Yasser Arafat, the challenges faced, and the tragic assassination of Yitzhak Rabin.

- Chapter 4: Roadmap to Peace: Navigate through the Second Intifada, the Arab Peace Initiative, the security barrier, and the Gaza Disengagement.

- Chapter 5: People-to-People Initiatives and Civil Society: Explore grassroots efforts, economic collaborations, interfaith dialogues, and the setbacks faced by civil society initiatives.

- Chapter 6: Ongoing Challenges and Regional Dynamics: Analyze the role of international mediation, shifting regional alliances, the rise of extremism, and the impacts of geopolitical shifts.

- Chapter 7: Human Stories and Resilience: Share personal narratives of conflict, amplify voices for peace and coexistence, delve into the resilience of communities, and highlight the role of women in peacebuilding.

- Chapter 8: The Elusive Peace and Potential for Conflict: Confront the continuing challenges, draw lessons from past peace initiatives, explore potential triggers for conflict, and emphasize the ongoing need for international involvement.

Conclusion:

In the concluding chapter, we will summarize the key takeaways, underscore the significance of persistent efforts for peace, encourage readers to engage actively with the issue, and contemplate the uncertain future of the Israeli-Palestinian conflict.

This book aspires to be more than a historical account; it aims to be a journey, an exploration, and a catalyst for deeper understanding. As we navigate the chapters that follow, let us embark on this expedition with an open mind and a commitment to unraveling the intricate tapestry of the Holy Land turmoil.

Establishing the importance of understanding the Israeli-Palestinian conflict and its potential for resolution is paramount as we embark on this exploration. This conflict, rooted in historical grievances and political complexities, extends far beyond the borders of the Holy Land, influencing regional dynamics and global geopolitics. To grasp its significance is to recognize its enduring impact on countless lives and the broader quest for global stability.

The Human Cost:

At the heart of this conflict lies a profound human cost. For decades, individuals on both sides have endured the consequences of violence, displacement, and the erosion of basic rights. Families have been torn apart, communities uprooted, and generations raised amidst the echoes of conflict. Understanding the depth of these human experiences is essential for fostering empathy and compassion, compelling us to seek a resolution that transcends political and ideological divides.

Regional Implications:

Beyond its immediate borders, the Israeli-Palestinian conflict reverberates throughout the Middle East and beyond. It has played a pivotal role in shaping regional alliances, influencing diplomatic relations, and impacting the stability of neighboring nations. The potential for resolution extends beyond individual grievances to the broader aim of cultivating a more stable and harmonious Middle East.

Global Security and Diplomacy:

The conflict's far-reaching implications extend to the global stage, affecting international security and diplomacy. The unresolved nature of the Israeli-Palestinian conflict has contributed to tensions, fueled extremism, and posed challenges to international efforts for peace. Recognizing its importance means acknowledging its role in shaping the geopolitical landscape and the interconnected nature of global security.

Cultural and Religious Significance:

The Holy Land holds profound cultural and religious significance for millions around the world. Understanding the conflict requires an appreciation of the diverse narratives and identities entwined within its soil. The potential for resolution is, therefore, not only a political necessity but a step towards preserving the cultural heritage and religious sanctity of the region.

Moral Imperative:

Beyond geopolitics and regional dynamics, there exists a moral imperative to address and understand the

Israeli-Palestinian conflict. It challenges our collective commitment to justice, human rights, and the pursuit of peace. Recognizing this imperative underscores the shared responsibility of the international community to contribute to efforts that seek a just and lasting resolution.

A Window of Opportunity:

While the conflict's complexities are undeniable, understanding it is also recognizing the potential for resolution. History has shown that dialogue, negotiation, and diplomacy can pave the way for peace. By understanding the nuances of the conflict, we empower ourselves to advocate for constructive solutions, support peace initiatives, and contribute to a future where both Israelis and Palestinians can coexist in dignity and security.

In setting the stage for this exploration, we acknowledge the importance of unraveling the layers of this conflict. To comprehend its intricacies is to recognize our shared responsibility in contributing to a world where the cycles of violence are replaced with the promise of a more peaceful and just future.

Chapter 1: Historical Roots of the Conflict
Ancient History and Shared Heritage

In unraveling the intricate tapestry of the Israeli-Palestinian conflict, we must first venture into the distant echoes of antiquity, where the roots of this multifaceted struggle are entwined with ancient history and a shared heritage. Understanding the historical context of the Holy Land is crucial for comprehending the complex layers of identities, narratives, and aspirations that converge within its borders.

Ancient History:

The history of the Holy Land is a narrative etched into the bedrock of time, marked by the footsteps of diverse civilizations. From the ancient Canaanites to the Babylonians, Persians, Greeks, and Romans, the region has been a crucible of cultural exchange, religious evolution, and territorial conquests. The intertwining histories of the indigenous peoples and successive empires form the backdrop against which the Israeli-Palestinian conflict unfolded.

The rise and fall of empires, the construction of ancient cities, and the emergence of monotheistic faiths all left indelible imprints on the land. Jerusalem, with its sacred sites revered by Jews, Christians, and Muslims alike, became a focal point of religious and cultural significance, laying the foundation for the shared heritage that shapes the present-day conflict.

Shared Heritage:

Within this mosaic of history emerges a shared heritage—a tapestry woven with threads of diverse cultures, languages, and traditions. The ancient Hebrews, Philistines, Canaanites, and later, the Byzantines and Ottomans, all contributed to the rich cultural fabric of the Holy Land. This shared heritage, however, is not a simple narrative of harmony; it is also a tale of coexistence amid periods of tension and conquest.

The Abrahamic faiths—Judaism, Christianity, and Islam—each find roots in this sacred soil, creating a shared spiritual heritage. The stories of Abraham, Moses, Jesus, and Muhammad intersect in the Holy Land, contributing to the deep connections and profound significance that this region holds for millions around the world.

Tensions and Coexistence:

Yet, this shared heritage is not without its tensions. Historical conflicts, territorial disputes, and the ebb and flow of empires have left enduring marks on the land. The Crusades, Mamluk rule, and the Ottoman era witnessed moments of coexistence and clashes, shaping the complex relationships between the diverse communities inhabiting the region.

Understanding the ancient history and shared heritage is essential for recognizing the diverse identities that have evolved over millennia. It provides a nuanced perspective on the complexities of the Israeli-Palestinian conflict, where historical narratives, religious symbolism, and territorial claims converge in a delicate dance.

As we delve into the annals of ancient history, we set the stage for comprehending the evolving dynamics of the Holy Land—a stage where the echoes of the past resonate in the present, laying the foundation for the chapters that follow.

British Mandate and the Birth of Israel

As we navigate the labyrinth of historical roots shaping the Israeli-Palestinian conflict, a pivotal chapter unfolds with the imposition of the British Mandate—a period that set in motion a cascade of events culminating in the birth of the State of Israel. This era, marked by geopolitical shifts and competing national aspirations, laid the groundwork for the complexities that continue to define the Holy Land.

The Aftermath of World War I:

The collapse of the Ottoman Empire at the end of World War I ushered in a new era for the Middle East. The League of Nations entrusted Britain with the administration of Palestine, a land whose destiny would be indelibly altered. The British Mandate, initially hailed with aspirations of fostering self-determination and development, quickly became a crucible of conflicting interests.

Zionism and the Balfour Declaration:

Against the backdrop of the Mandate, the Zionist movement gained momentum. The Balfour Declaration of 1917, a pivotal moment in the shaping of the conflict, expressed British support for the establishment of a "national home for the Jewish people" in Palestine. This declaration, while celebrated by the Zionist movement, sowed the seeds of tension with the Palestinian Arab population, setting the stage for the struggles to come.

Arab-Jewish Tensions:

As Jewish immigration increased under the Mandate, tensions between Arab and Jewish communities intensified. Competing national aspirations and claims to the same land fueled clashes, protests, and a sense of foreboding that the region was hurtling toward a tumultuous future. The emergence of distinct national identities, Arab and Jewish, became more pronounced, setting the stage for the birth of two separate nations.

White Papers and Restrictive Policies:

British attempts to navigate the complexities of the Mandate through a series of White Papers sought to balance the competing demands of Arabs and Jews. However, these policies often fell short of appeasing either side, deepening mistrust and animosity. Restrictive immigration quotas and land allocation policies exacerbated tensions, creating a volatile atmosphere in which both communities vied for control and recognition.

The Birth of Israel:

The aftermath of World War II witnessed a pivotal moment—the Holocaust, which catalyzed international support for the establishment of a Jewish homeland. The

United Nations, succeeding the League of Nations, proposed the partition of Palestine into separate Jewish and Arab states, with Jerusalem as an international city. In 1948, against a backdrop of jubilation for one community and despair for another, the State of Israel was proclaimed.

The Nakba:

However, the declaration of Israel resulted in a catastrophic exodus for the Palestinian Arab population, a mass displacement known as the Nakba or "catastrophe." Hundreds of thousands of Palestinians were uprooted from their homes, creating a refugee crisis that persists to this day. The Nakba became a defining moment in Palestinian collective memory, shaping their narrative of dispossession and longing for return.

The chapter of the British Mandate and the birth of Israel is a pivotal juncture in the narrative of the Israeli-Palestinian conflict. It is a tale of divergent national aspirations, international interventions, and the forging of identities that would fuel the struggles of the ensuing decades. As we move forward in our exploration, the echoes of this chapter resonate, shaping the contours of the conflict's historical landscape.

Palestinian Displacement (Nakba)

In the annals of the Israeli-Palestinian conflict, the chapter titled "Palestinian Displacement," often referred to as the Nakba or "catastrophe," stands as a haunting testament to the profound human cost of geopolitical decisions and shifting borders. This seismic event, following the declaration of the State of Israel in 1948, reshaped the demographic and political landscape of the Holy Land, leaving an indelible mark on generations of Palestinians.

The Context of the Nakba:

The Nakba was not a singular event but a culmination of historical forces, geopolitical decisions, and the deepening tensions between Jewish and Arab communities in Palestine. As the State of Israel was proclaimed, the Arab-Israeli War of 1948 unfolded, becoming a crucible of conflict and displacement. The Nakba represents the mass exodus of hundreds of thousands of Palestinians from their homes—a harrowing experience that reverberates through Palestinian collective memory.

The Exodus and Refugee Crisis:

As the conflict intensified, Palestinian Arab communities found themselves caught in the crossfire, facing displacement on an unprecedented scale. Fleeing violence, coercion, and a prevailing sense of insecurity, Palestinians sought refuge in neighboring Arab countries or found themselves in makeshift camps. The refugee crisis became a defining feature of the Nakba, with displaced families grappling with the loss of homes, livelihoods, and a sense of belonging.

Roots of Displacement:

The roots of Palestinian displacement can be traced to a combination of factors. The military advances of Israeli forces, accompanied by strategic expulsions and a climate of fear, compelled many Palestinians to leave their homes. Additionally, the breakdown of local ceasefires and the broader context of regional hostilities contributed to the unfolding tragedy. Villages and towns that had thrived for generations became deserted landscapes, symbolizing the profound rupture caused by the Nakba.

Impact on Palestinian Society:

The Nakba had far-reaching consequences for Palestinian society. Families were torn apart, communities fragmented, and a rich cultural tapestry was irrevocably altered. The dispersion of Palestinians across different countries created a diaspora that retained a collective longing for return—a central theme in Palestinian identity and aspirations. The trauma of the Nakba became a shaping force, influencing the narratives, poetry, and cultural expressions of a dispossessed people.

The Right of Return:

Central to the Nakba narrative is the right of return—the belief among Palestinians that they have a right to return to the homes and lands from which they were displaced. This principle, enshrined in international law, has been a consistent point of contention in peace negotiations and a key factor in the persistence of the Israeli-Palestinian conflict.

Legacy and Contested Narratives:

The Nakba is not merely a historical event but a living legacy that continues to shape the discourse surrounding the Israeli-Palestinian conflict. The narratives of the Nakba are contested, reflecting the deep divisions and differing perspectives on the historical realities and responsibilities that led to the displacement.

As we delve into the Nakba, we confront a chapter of profound sorrow and enduring consequence. It is a story of displacement, dispossession, and the profound human toll exacted by the turbulence of historical forces. The echoes of the Nakba resonate through the chapters that follow, casting a long shadow on the Israeli-Palestinian conflict's historical landscape.

The Six-Day War of 1967 stands as a pivotal chapter in the Israeli-Palestinian conflict, a seismic event that not only redrew the map of the Middle East but also left a lasting impact on the dynamics of the Holy Land. This conflict, lasting only six days, would have profound implications, giving rise to an occupation that has endured for decades and remains a central point of contention in the ongoing struggle.

Origins and Escalation:

The roots of the Six-Day War can be traced to rising tensions between Israel and its Arab neighbors, particularly Egypt and Syria. Disputes over borders, access to water resources, and the broader Arab-Israeli conflict set the stage for a regional conflagration. In June 1967, a series of events, including the closing of the Straits of Tiran by Egypt and the massing of troops on Israel's borders, led to a rapid escalation.

The Lightning War:

The conflict unfolded with unprecedented speed and intensity. Israeli forces launched a preemptive strike on June 5, 1967, targeting airfields and military installations. What ensued was a lightning war, characterized by swift and decisive Israeli military victories on multiple fronts. By June

10, Israel had gained control of the Sinai Peninsula, the West Bank, East Jerusalem, and the Golan Heights.

Occupation of the West Bank and East Jerusalem:

One of the defining outcomes of the Six-Day War was the Israeli occupation of the West Bank and East Jerusalem. The ancient city of Jerusalem, revered by Jews, Christians, and Muslims alike, came under Israeli control. This shift in sovereignty marked a profound change in the status quo, igniting a complex web of political, religious, and cultural implications.

Settlement Expansion and Controversies:

In the aftermath of the war, Israel embarked on a policy of settlement expansion in the newly occupied territories. Jewish settlements were established in the West Bank and East Jerusalem, leading to a protracted and contentious issue. The construction of settlements, considered illegal under international law, became a source of tension and a major obstacle to peace negotiations.

Impact on Palestinian Identity:

The occupation profoundly influenced the trajectory of Palestinian identity. The territories captured in 1967 became the focal point of Palestinian aspirations for statehood. The occupation gave rise to a new chapter in the Palestinian struggle, with resistance movements, intifadas, and a quest for self-determination becoming defining features of the Palestinian national narrative.

International Response and UN Resolutions:

The international community responded to the occupation with a series of United Nations resolutions, condemning Israel's actions and calling for the withdrawal from the occupied territories. However, the implementation of these resolutions has proven challenging, and the occupation persists, contributing to ongoing tensions and challenges in the pursuit of peace.

The East Jerusalem Conundrum:

The status of East Jerusalem, with its religious significance and cultural heritage, remains a particularly contentious aspect of the occupation. The annexation of East Jerusalem by Israel has not been recognized by the international community, and the city remains a focal point of diplomatic disputes and negotiations.

Legacy and Ongoing Implications:

The Six-Day War and its aftermath continue to shape the contours of the Israeli-Palestinian conflict. The occupation has endured for over five decades, becoming a central point of contention in peace negotiations and a source of enduring grievances. The legacy of the war looms large, casting a shadow over the prospects for a just and lasting resolution to the complex and deeply rooted conflict.

Chapter 2: Early Peace Initiatives
United Nations Resolutions

In the aftermath of the Six-Day War, the international community faced the formidable task of addressing the complex and volatile situation in the Middle East. This period saw the initiation of early peace initiatives, with the United Nations (UN) playing a central role in attempting to forge a path towards stability and resolution. The examination of United Nations resolutions during this critical juncture offers insights into the evolving diplomatic landscape and the challenges faced in navigating the intricate dynamics of the Israeli-Palestinian conflict.

The UN and the Aftermath of the Six-Day War:

As the guns fell silent in the wake of the Six-Day War, the United Nations found itself at the forefront of international efforts to address the consequences of the conflict. The rapid territorial changes, displacement of populations, and the occupation of strategic territories prompted urgent diplomatic action. The UN Security Council became a crucial arena for deliberations, resolutions, and attempts to chart a course towards peace.

Resolution 242: The Land for Peace Principle:

Central to early UN efforts was Security Council Resolution 242, adopted on November 22, 1967. This landmark resolution called for the withdrawal of Israeli armed forces from territories occupied during the Six-Day War and emphasized the principle of "land for peace." The resolution laid the groundwork for subsequent diplomatic initiatives and became a cornerstone for future peace negotiations.

Implementation Challenges:

While Resolution 242 outlined a framework for addressing the territorial aspects of the conflict, its implementation faced significant challenges. The intricacies of withdrawal, the status of Jerusalem, the right of return for Palestinian refugees, and the establishment of secure and recognized boundaries became contentious issues. The resolution's ambiguity regarding the specifics of withdrawal left room for interpretation and disagreement, contributing to ongoing tensions.

Resolution 338 and the Yom Kippur War:

The Yom Kippur War of 1973 led to the adoption of Security Council Resolution 338 on October 22, 1973. This resolution called for an immediate ceasefire and urged the implementation of Resolution 242. The Yom Kippur War underscored the fragility of the regional balance and the need for sustained international engagement to prevent further escalation.

The Geneva Conference and the Stalemate:

In the aftermath of the Yom Kippur War, diplomatic efforts intensified. The United States and the Soviet Union jointly convened the Geneva Conference in December 1973, bringing together key stakeholders, including Israel, Egypt, and Syria. However, the conference failed to yield substantive results, highlighting the complexity of addressing the multifaceted issues at the heart of the conflict.

The Palestinian Question and UN Recognition:

During this period, the Palestinian question emerged as a central aspect of diplomatic discourse. UN General Assembly Resolution 3236, adopted in 1974, recognized the Palestinian people's right to self-determination, statehood, and sovereignty. The resolution marked a shift in the international approach to the Palestinian cause, acknowledging the need for a political solution that addressed the aspirations of the Palestinian people.

UN Security Council Resolution 338: Camp David and Beyond:

Security Council Resolution 338 remained a focal point for diplomatic efforts. It played a role in subsequent peace negotiations, including the Camp David Accords between Israel and Egypt in 1978. The accords, facilitated by the United States, resulted in the first-ever peace treaty between Israel and an Arab state but did not comprehensively address the Palestinian question.

Conclusion and Legacy:

The examination of United Nations resolutions during the early peace initiatives underscores the complexity of addressing the Israeli-Palestinian conflict. While these resolutions laid foundational principles, the challenges of implementation, competing narratives, and evolving geopolitical dynamics continued to shape the trajectory of the conflict. The legacy of these early UN initiatives remains embedded in the ongoing quest for a just and lasting resolution to the complexities of the Israeli-Palestinian conflict.

Suez Crisis and Suez Canal Crisis

In the complex tapestry of early peace initiatives in the Middle East, the Suez Crisis and the associated Suez Canal Crisis emerged as critical chapters that not only reshaped regional dynamics but also laid the groundwork for subsequent diplomatic efforts. The events surrounding the Suez Crisis, spanning from 1956 to 1957, revealed the intricate interplay of global powers, regional aspirations, and the complexities of addressing the Israeli-Palestinian conflict.

Origins of the Crisis:

The roots of the Suez Crisis can be traced to a convergence of factors, including the nationalization of the Suez Canal by Egyptian President Gamal Abdel Nasser in 1956. Nasser's decision to assert control over this vital waterway sparked international tensions, particularly with Britain and France, who viewed the move as a threat to their strategic interests in the region.

The Role of Israel:

Against this backdrop, a complex web of diplomatic maneuvering unfolded. Israel, sensing an opportunity to address its security concerns and weaken Nasser, formed a secret alliance with Britain and France. In October 1956, Israeli forces invaded the Sinai Peninsula, swiftly advancing towards the Suez Canal. The coordinated military actions of the three nations marked the beginning of the Suez Crisis.

International Response and U.S. Involvement:

The actions of Britain, France, and Israel drew swift condemnation from the international community. The United States, under President Dwight D. Eisenhower, played a pivotal role in defusing the crisis. The Eisenhower administration, concerned about Cold War dynamics and the potential for escalating tensions, exerted diplomatic pressure on its traditional allies, leading to a withdrawal of forces by the aggressors.

United Nations Intervention:

The Suez Crisis became a defining moment for the United Nations as it demonstrated the organization's potential as a mediator in conflicts. The General Assembly and the Security Council convened to address the crisis. The United Nations Emergency Force (UNEF) was subsequently deployed to supervise the withdrawal of foreign forces from Egypt and ensure stability in the region.

Impact on the Palestinian Question:

While the Suez Crisis itself did not directly address the Israeli-Palestinian conflict, its aftermath had a profound impact on the broader regional dynamics. The crisis elevated the Palestinian cause on the international stage, with the establishment of the Palestine Liberation Organization (PLO) in 1964. The PLO emerged as a key player in articulating Palestinian aspirations and seeking a resolution to the conflict.

Legacy and Lessons Learned:

The Suez Crisis left a lasting imprint on diplomatic strategies in the Middle East. The international community, particularly the United States, recognized the importance of addressing the root causes of regional tensions, including the Israeli-Palestinian conflict, to maintain stability. The crisis served as a lesson in the limitations of military interventions and the necessity of diplomatic solutions.

The Suez Canal Crisis of 1967:

The Suez Canal Crisis of 1967, also known as the Second Arab-Israeli War or the Six-Day War, marked another tumultuous chapter in the region's history. The closure of the Suez Canal by Egypt and heightened military tensions led to a swift and decisive conflict. Israel, in a pre-emptive strike, achieved significant territorial gains, including the Sinai Peninsula and the Gaza Strip, further altering the landscape of the Israeli-Palestinian conflict.

Conclusion:

The Suez Crisis and its subsequent iterations underscored the complex interplay of geopolitical interests, regional dynamics, and the interconnectedness of conflicts in the Middle East. The events surrounding the Suez Crisis laid bare the challenges of addressing the Israeli-Palestinian conflict within a broader context and set the stage for evolving diplomatic initiatives in the quest for lasting peace.

Camp David Accords

In the annals of Middle East diplomacy, the Camp David Accords of 1978 represent a historic milestone—an ambitious endeavor to forge a framework for peace between Egypt and Israel. This chapter in the early peace initiatives not only transformed regional dynamics but also brought the Israeli-Palestinian conflict to the forefront of international attention. The examination of the Camp David Accords offers insights into the intricate negotiations, the complexities of the peace process, and the challenges of addressing the multifaceted aspects of the Israeli-Palestinian conflict.

The Genesis of Camp David:

The seeds of the Camp David Accords were sown against the backdrop of the Yom Kippur War in 1973, which underscored the need for diplomatic solutions to prevent further conflict. President Anwar Sadat of Egypt and Prime Minister Menachem Begin of Israel, under the mediation of U.S. President Jimmy Carter, embarked on a path of diplomatic engagement to explore possibilities for peace.

The Camp David Summit:

The Camp David Summit, held at the presidential retreat in Maryland from September 5 to 17, 1978, marked a pivotal moment in the quest for peace. The negotiations, characterized by intense and protracted discussions, sought to address key issues, including the status of the Sinai Peninsula, security arrangements, and the question of Palestinian autonomy.

The Framework for Peace:

The culmination of the summit was the Camp David Accords, a framework for peace between Egypt and Israel. The accords consisted of two main documents: the Framework for Peace in the Middle East and the Framework for the Conclusion of a Peace Treaty between Egypt and Israel. These documents outlined the principles for the withdrawal of Israeli forces from the Sinai Peninsula, the normalization of relations between Egypt and Israel, and the commitment to address the Palestinian question.

Addressing the Palestinian Question:

While the Camp David Accords focused primarily on the Egyptian-Israeli relationship, they also recognized the importance of addressing the broader Palestinian question. The accords called for negotiations to determine the future status of the West Bank and Gaza Strip, acknowledging the need for autonomy for the Palestinian people. However, the specifics of Palestinian self-rule were left for subsequent negotiations.

Controversies and Criticisms:

The Camp David Accords were not without controversies and criticisms. While hailed as a breakthrough, particularly in Egyptian-Israeli relations, the accords faced opposition from some Arab nations and Palestinian factions. Critics argued that the accords did not adequately address the rights and aspirations of the Palestinian people and that the autonomy envisioned fell short of a comprehensive solution.

Implementation Challenges:

The implementation of the Camp David Accords faced considerable challenges. The process of negotiating a comprehensive peace treaty proved intricate, with issues such as the status of Jerusalem, Israeli settlements, and the delineation of borders becoming contentious points. The complexities of the Israeli-Palestinian conflict became increasingly evident as negotiations moved forward.

The Egypt-Israel Peace Treaty:

Despite the challenges, the momentum generated at Camp David ultimately led to the signing of the Egypt-Israel Peace Treaty on March 26, 1979. The treaty marked the first time an Arab nation formally recognized Israel, and, in return, Israel withdrew from the Sinai Peninsula. The peace treaty between Egypt and Israel was a groundbreaking achievement, but it did not address the broader Israeli-Palestinian conflict.

Legacy and Lessons Learned:

The Camp David Accords left a lasting legacy in Middle East diplomacy. The accords demonstrated that peace between longtime adversaries was possible through sustained diplomatic efforts. However, the complexities of the Israeli-Palestinian conflict persisted, and the accords highlighted the need for a comprehensive approach to address the multifaceted issues at the heart of the broader regional dynamics.

Conclusion:

The Camp David Accords represented a significant chapter in the early peace initiatives in the Middle East. While they successfully addressed the Egyptian-Israeli relationship and set a precedent for diplomatic engagement, the unresolved issues pertaining to the Israeli-Palestinian conflict underscored the intricate challenges of achieving a comprehensive and lasting peace in the region. The accords, nonetheless, laid the groundwork for subsequent diplomatic efforts and remain a landmark in the quest for stability and resolution in the Middle East.

Beginnings of Palestinian Liberation Movements

The emergence of Palestinian Liberation Movements marks a crucial chapter in the historical narrative of the Israeli-Palestinian conflict. These movements, driven by a desire for self-determination, justice, and the establishment of an independent Palestinian state, have played a significant role in shaping the trajectory of the conflict. Exploring the beginnings of Palestinian Liberation Movements unveils a complex tapestry of political, social, and historical dynamics that have deeply influenced the quest for Palestinian rights and statehood.

The Historical Context:

The roots of Palestinian Liberation Movements can be traced to the aftermath of the Nakba in 1948, a period marked by the mass displacement of Palestinians and the establishment of the State of Israel. The dispossession and the longing for a homeland galvanized Palestinian communities, giving rise to collective aspirations for liberation and the right of return.

Formation of the Palestine Liberation Organization (PLO):

The Palestine Liberation Organization (PLO) stands as a central and pioneering force among Palestinian Liberation Movements. Founded in 1964, the PLO aimed to unite various Palestinian factions under a single umbrella organization. Its charter articulated the goal of liberating Palestine and establishing an independent state. The PLO became a key actor in the international arena, representing the Palestinian cause and advocating for self-determination.

Fatah and Yasser Arafat:

Within the PLO, the Fatah movement, led by Yasser Arafat, emerged as a dominant force. Fatah played a crucial role in shaping the military and political strategies of the PLO. Arafat, a charismatic and emblematic leader, became the face of the Palestinian resistance. Fatah's influence extended beyond military operations, emphasizing diplomatic efforts and international recognition.

Armed Struggle and Guerrilla Warfare:

The early years of Palestinian Liberation Movements were characterized by armed struggle and guerrilla warfare. The fedayeen, or Palestinian guerrilla fighters, engaged in armed resistance against Israeli forces. High-profile operations, such as the Battle of Karameh in 1968, showcased the determination of Palestinian fighters and brought the Palestinian cause to global attention.

International Support and Recognition:

The activism of Palestinian Liberation Movements garnered international support, particularly from Arab nations and non-aligned countries. The Palestinian cause became a focal point in regional and global forums, with the United Nations recognizing the PLO as the legitimate representative of the Palestinian people in 1974. This diplomatic milestone elevated the status of Palestinian Liberation Movements on the international stage.

The Role of Popular Front for the Liberation of Palestine (PFLP) and Other Factions:

The Popular Front for the Liberation of Palestine (PFLP), led by George Habash, and other factions within the PLO contributed diverse ideological perspectives to the Palestinian struggle. The PFLP, known for its Marxist-Leninist orientation, engaged in both armed resistance and political advocacy. The multiplicity of factions within the PLO reflected the diversity of Palestinian society and political thought.

The Impact of the Oslo Accords:

The signing of the Oslo Accords in 1993 marked a pivotal moment in the trajectory of Palestinian Liberation Movements. The accords led to the establishment of the Palestinian Authority (PA) and a degree of self-governance in parts of the West Bank and Gaza Strip. While this represented a step toward Palestinian statehood, it also sparked internal divisions within the Palestinian political landscape.

Challenges and Internal Divisions:

Over the years, Palestinian Liberation Movements faced internal divisions, ideological differences, and challenges in articulating a unified strategy. The Oslo Accords and subsequent developments, including the failure of peace talks and the continuation of Israeli settlements, contributed to internal dissent and debates within the Palestinian political arena.

The Second Intifada:

The Second Intifada, a period of intensified Palestinian uprising from 2000 to 2005, reflected the frustration and grievances of Palestinians. While characterized by mass protests and acts of civil disobedience, it also witnessed armed confrontations between Palestinian militants and Israeli forces. The Second Intifada underscored the complexities of achieving a just and lasting resolution to the conflict.

Legacy and Continuing Struggle:

The legacy of Palestinian Liberation Movements endures as a testament to the resilience and determination of the Palestinian people. Despite internal challenges, shifting geopolitical dynamics, and evolving strategies, the quest for self-determination and statehood remains a central theme. Palestinian Liberation Movements continue to navigate the complexities of the Israeli-Palestinian conflict, advocating for the rights and aspirations of the Palestinian people on the global stage.

Conclusion:

The beginnings of Palestinian Liberation Movements embody a multifaceted journey marked by resistance, diplomacy, and the pursuit of justice. From the establishment of the PLO to the varied approaches of factions within, these movements have been central in shaping the discourse around the Israeli-Palestinian conflict. As the struggle for Palestinian rights continues, the legacy of these movements remains an integral part of the ongoing quest for a just and lasting resolution in the Middle East.

Chapter 3: Oslo Accords and the Peace Process
Oslo Accords and the Declaration of Principles

The Oslo Accords and the Declaration of Principles (DOP) represent a watershed moment in the Israeli-Palestinian conflict, offering a framework for peace negotiations and the prospect of a two-state solution. This chapter delves into the intricacies of the Oslo Accords, examining the historical context, the negotiations that led to the accords, and the aspirations for peace that accompanied this landmark agreement.

Historical Context:

The Oslo Accords emerged against the backdrop of decades of conflict and failed attempts at resolution. The First Intifada, which began in 1987, highlighted the need for a new approach to address the grievances of both Palestinians and Israelis. Secret negotiations, facilitated by Norway, laid the groundwork for a groundbreaking agreement that sought to chart a path towards coexistence.

The Secret Negotiations:

The Oslo process began with secret negotiations in Oslo, Norway, between Israeli and Palestinian representatives. The participants included figures such as Yossi Beilin and Yair Hirschfeld on the Israeli side and Ahmed Qurei and Abu Ala (Ahmed Nasser) representing the

Palestinians. These early talks set the stage for the formal negotiations that would follow.

Declaration of Principles (DOP):

The Oslo Accords were officially signed on the White House lawn on September 13, 1993, marking a historic handshake between Israeli Prime Minister Yitzhak Rabin and Palestine Liberation Organization (PLO) Chairman Yasser Arafat, with U.S. President Bill Clinton as a witness. The foundational document of the Oslo Accords was the Declaration of Principles.

Key Principles of the DOP:

The Declaration of Principles outlined key principles that formed the basis for subsequent negotiations. These principles included the recognition of the mutual legitimate political rights of both Palestinians and Israelis, the establishment of a Palestinian interim self-government in parts of the West Bank and Gaza Strip, and the commitment to negotiate a permanent status agreement within five years.

Interim Period and the Establishment of the Palestinian Authority:

The Oslo Accords ushered in an interim period during which the Palestinian Authority (PA) was established to govern parts of the West Bank and Gaza. Yasser Arafat assumed the role of president of the PA, and a Palestinian

Legislative Council was formed. The PA took responsibility for certain civil affairs, and Palestinian police forces were deployed.

Challenges and Setbacks:

While the Oslo Accords represented a significant breakthrough, they also faced immediate challenges. Issues such as the status of Jerusalem, the right of return for Palestinian refugees, and the future borders of a Palestinian state remained contentious. Moreover, acts of violence and terrorism threatened the fragile peace process.

The Role of the United States and International Community:

The United States, under the Clinton administration, played a pivotal role in facilitating and supporting the Oslo Accords. The international community welcomed the prospects of peace and invested diplomatic efforts in supporting the negotiations. However, challenges arose as the negotiations progressed, and the complexities of the Israeli-Palestinian conflict became increasingly evident.

Assassination of Yitzhak Rabin:

The assassination of Israeli Prime Minister Yitzhak Rabin in 1995 by a Jewish extremist further complicated the peace process. Rabin, who had been a key architect of the Oslo Accords, was succeeded by Benjamin Netanyahu, whose government had a different approach to the peace negotiations.

Continued Negotiations and Wye River Memorandum:

Despite setbacks, negotiations continued with the signing of the Wye River Memorandum in 1998. This interim agreement aimed to address outstanding issues and facilitate further Israeli withdrawals from parts of the West Bank. However, the implementation of the Wye River Memorandum faced challenges, and the prospects of a final status agreement remained elusive.

Legacy and Criticisms:

The legacy of the Oslo Accords is complex and subject to debate. While the accords marked a historic attempt at resolving the Israeli-Palestinian conflict, criticisms have been levied regarding the lack of progress on key issues, the impact on Palestinian sovereignty, and the failure to achieve a final status agreement within the envisioned timeframe.

Conclusion:

The Oslo Accords and the Declaration of Principles represented a groundbreaking effort to bring about a negotiated resolution to the Israeli-Palestinian conflict. The accords signaled a willingness on both sides to engage in dialogue and seek common ground. However, the road to a comprehensive peace proved challenging, and the Oslo process left a complex legacy with enduring implications for the ongoing quest for a just and lasting resolution in the Middle East.

The Role of Yasser Arafat

Yasser Arafat, the charismatic and controversial leader of the Palestine Liberation Organization (PLO), played a pivotal role in the Oslo Accords and the broader peace process between Israelis and Palestinians. This section examines Arafat's leadership, his involvement in the Oslo negotiations, and the complexities of his role in shaping the trajectory of the Israeli-Palestinian conflict during this critical period.

Early Years and Formation of the PLO:

Born in 1929 in Cairo, Egypt, Yasser Arafat emerged as a key figure in the Palestinian national movement. Arafat played a prominent role in the establishment of the Fatah movement in the late 1950s, which later became a leading faction within the PLO. The PLO, founded in 1964, sought to represent the Palestinian people and their aspirations for self-determination.

Arafat's Leadership Style:

Yasser Arafat's leadership style was characterized by a blend of revolutionary fervor, political pragmatism, and a keen understanding of the complexities of the Palestinian struggle. Arafat's charisma and ability to navigate shifting geopolitical landscapes contributed to his role as the face of the Palestinian cause on the international stage.

The PLO's Shift Towards Diplomacy:

As the head of the PLO, Arafat led the organization through various phases, including armed struggle and diplomatic initiatives. The recognition of the PLO by the United Nations in 1974 marked a diplomatic milestone, acknowledging the organization as the legitimate representative of the Palestinian people. Arafat's address to the UN General Assembly further elevated the Palestinian cause in global discourse.

Involvement in Armed Resistance:

Arafat's involvement in armed resistance against Israel, particularly during the 1970s and 1980s, shaped the perception of the PLO as a key player in the struggle for Palestinian rights. The organization's militant activities included high-profile incidents, such as the Munich Olympics hostage crisis in 1972, which drew international attention to the Palestinian cause.

The Oslo Accords: Arafat's Strategic Pivot:

The Oslo Accords marked a significant strategic shift for Arafat and the PLO. The secret negotiations in Oslo, facilitated by Norway, led to the historic handshake between Arafat and Israeli Prime Minister Yitzhak Rabin on the White House lawn in 1993. Arafat's decision to engage in direct negotiations with Israel reflected a willingness to explore diplomatic avenues for the resolution of the conflict.

The Signing Ceremony and Arafat's Speech:

The signing ceremony of the Oslo Accords on September 13, 1993, became an iconic moment in the history of the Israeli-Palestinian conflict. Arafat, clad in his trademark keffiyeh, delivered a speech expressing hope for a new era of peace. His words emphasized the need for coexistence and the establishment of a Palestinian state.

Challenges and Criticisms:

Arafat's engagement in the peace process faced internal challenges and criticisms. Some factions within the PLO, including elements of Fatah, opposed the Oslo Accords, viewing them as a compromise that did not adequately address Palestinian rights. Arafat's leadership style, characterized by a degree of centralized control, drew criticism for marginalizing dissenting voices.

Implementation of the Oslo Accords:

Arafat assumed a central role in implementing the Oslo Accords, overseeing the establishment of the Palestinian Authority (PA) and its institutions. The PA assumed governance responsibilities in parts of the West Bank and Gaza Strip. Arafat himself became the first president of the PA, solidifying his position as the leader of the embryonic Palestinian self-governance entity.

The Peace Process and Stumbling Blocks:

As the peace process unfolded, Arafat faced formidable challenges. The unresolved status of Jerusalem, the right of return for Palestinian refugees, and the question of Israeli settlements became major stumbling blocks. Arafat's leadership was tested as the negotiations encountered obstacles, and the timeline for achieving a final status agreement proved elusive.

Camp David Summit and Aftermath:

The Camp David Summit in 2000, facilitated by U.S. President Bill Clinton, aimed to address final status issues. However, the summit ended without a comprehensive agreement. The subsequent outbreak of the Second Intifada in 2000 presented a severe test of Arafat's leadership, with accusations of failed negotiations and questions about his ability to control the situation.

Legacy and Controversies:

Yasser Arafat's legacy remains a subject of controversy and debate. While recognized as a symbol of Palestinian resistance and statehood aspirations, his leadership is also scrutinized for the challenges and setbacks in the peace process. Arafat's death in 2004, amid allegations of corruption and questions surrounding the circumstances of his illness, added layers of complexity to his legacy.

Conclusion:

Yasser Arafat's role in the Oslo Accords and the peace process marked a critical juncture in the history of the Israeli-Palestinian conflict. His leadership, characterized by a strategic pivot from armed resistance to diplomacy, had profound implications for the Palestinian cause. Arafat's complex legacy reflects the challenges, compromises, and aspirations entwined in the quest for a just and lasting resolution in the Middle East.

The Oslo Accords, heralded as a historic attempt to resolve the Israeli-Palestinian conflict, were not immune to challenges and setbacks. This section delves into the multifaceted difficulties that beset the peace process, examining internal and external factors that impeded progress, tested the resilience of the accords, and contributed to the protracted nature of the conflict.

Immediate Challenges Following the Oslo Accords:

While the Oslo Accords were signed with optimism and international acclaim, immediate challenges emerged, threatening the delicate balance struck between Israelis and Palestinians. Key issues, such as the status of Jerusalem, the right of return for Palestinian refugees, the delineation of borders, and the fate of Israeli settlements, became contentious points that foreshadowed the complexities of the negotiations.

Israeli Settlements:

The issue of Israeli settlements in the West Bank and Gaza Strip emerged as a persistent and contentious challenge. The Oslo Accords did not explicitly address the status of existing settlements or their expansion. The continued construction of settlements, viewed by

Palestinians as a violation of the accords, created tensions and eroded trust between the parties.

Jerusalem:

The status of Jerusalem, a city considered holy by Jews, Christians, and Muslims, proved to be an intractable issue. Both Israelis and Palestinians asserted historical and religious ties to the city, leading to deep-rooted disagreements. The Oslo Accords deferred the discussion on Jerusalem to later stages, leaving this critical issue unresolved.

Right of Return:

The right of return for Palestinian refugees displaced during the 1948 Arab-Israeli war was a deeply sensitive and unresolved issue. The Oslo Accords did not provide a clear framework for addressing the refugee question, leading to ongoing disputes over the rights and compensation of Palestinian refugees and their descendants.

Assassination of Yitzhak Rabin:

The assassination of Israeli Prime Minister Yitzhak Rabin in 1995 by a Jewish extremist, Yigal Amir, marked a tragic turning point in the peace process. Rabin, a key proponent of the Oslo Accords, was succeeded by Benjamin Netanyahu, whose government held a different approach to the negotiations. The assassination introduced uncertainty and instability into the peace process.

Netanyahu Era and Challenges to the Peace Process:

The election of Benjamin Netanyahu as Israeli Prime Minister in 1996 brought a shift in the dynamics of the peace process. Netanyahu, skeptical of the Oslo framework, advocated for a slower pace of negotiations and raised concerns about the security implications of Palestinian self-governance. The strained relationship between the Netanyahu government and the Palestinian Authority contributed to a stagnation in the peace process.

Failure of the Camp David Summit (2000):

The Camp David Summit in 2000, hosted by U.S. President Bill Clinton, aimed to address final status issues, including the status of Jerusalem and the right of return. The summit, however, ended without a comprehensive agreement. The failure of Camp David intensified mutual mistrust and frustration, laying the groundwork for the outbreak of the Second Intifada.

Second Intifada: Escalation of Violence and Setbacks:

The Second Intifada, a period of intensified Palestinian uprising from 2000 to 2005, marked a significant setback to the peace process. The breakdown of negotiations, combined with the visit of Israeli opposition leader Ariel Sharon to the Temple Mount, contributed to widespread protests, violence, and acts of terrorism. The subsequent Israeli military response further strained relations and hindered diplomatic efforts.

Erosion of Public Support and Trust:

As the peace process faced challenges, public support and trust eroded on both sides. Incidents of violence, broken promises, and unfulfilled expectations contributed to a sense of disillusionment among Palestinians and Israelis alike. The loss of confidence in the peace process complicated subsequent negotiations and the prospects for mutual understanding.

Divisions within Palestinian Society:

The Oslo Accords and their aftermath exposed internal divisions within Palestinian society. While some factions supported the peace process, others, including elements within Fatah and more radical groups, opposed what they perceived as compromising Palestinian rights. These internal divisions weakened the unified Palestinian stance in negotiations.

Continued Expansion of Settlements:

The continued expansion of Israeli settlements in the West Bank remained a persistent obstacle to the peace process. Despite international criticism and calls for a freeze on settlement construction, the expansion continued, altering the demographic and territorial landscape and complicating efforts to establish a viable Palestinian state.

International Dynamics and Changing Leadership:

Shifts in international dynamics and changes in leadership further complicated the peace process. The involvement of multiple international actors, each with its own interests and priorities, introduced additional layers of complexity. Changes in leadership both within Israel and the Palestinian Authority influenced the tone and direction of negotiations.

Legacy of the Oslo Accords:

The legacy of the Oslo Accords is one of mixed outcomes. While the accords represented a historic attempt at reconciliation, the unresolved issues, ongoing conflicts, and setbacks underscored the deep-seated challenges inherent in the quest for a lasting resolution to the Israeli-Palestinian conflict.

Conclusion:

Challenges and setbacks in the Oslo Accords and the peace process highlight the formidable obstacles that have impeded progress toward a comprehensive resolution. From the immediate aftermath of the accords to the complexities of final status negotiations, the Israeli-Palestinian conflict has remained a protracted and multifaceted challenge, reflecting the intricate nature of the issues at stake. Understanding the obstacles faced by negotiators and the consequences of setbacks is crucial for comprehending the complexities of the ongoing pursuit of peace in the region.

The Assassination of Yitzhak Rabin

The assassination of Israeli Prime Minister Yitzhak Rabin on November 4, 1995, sent shockwaves through the fragile landscape of the Israeli-Palestinian peace process initiated by the Oslo Accords. This section explores the life and leadership of Yitzhak Rabin, the circumstances leading to his tragic death, and the profound impact of this event on the trajectory of the peace process.

Yitzhak Rabin: Soldier, Statesman, Peacemaker:

Yitzhak Rabin's journey from a military career to becoming a statesman and peacemaker is integral to understanding the significance of his leadership. Born in Jerusalem in 1922, Rabin played pivotal roles in the Israeli military, commanding during the 1967 Six-Day War and later serving as Chief of Staff. His military prowess earned him respect, but it was his transition to politics that defined the latter part of his career.

The Oslo Accords and Rabin's Commitment to Peace:

Rabin's commitment to peace manifested prominently during his second term as Prime Minister, when he engaged in negotiations with the Palestinians leading to the Oslo Accords. The historic handshake between Rabin and PLO Chairman Yasser Arafat on the White House lawn in 1993 symbolized a significant breakthrough, with Rabin declaring a commitment to forging a new era of peaceful coexistence.

Internal Opposition and Right-Wing Criticism:

Rabin's pursuit of peace faced significant opposition within Israel. A segment of the Israeli population, particularly right-wing nationalists, viewed the Oslo Accords as a dangerous compromise that jeopardized Israel's security. The political climate became increasingly polarized, with Rabin facing criticism and even accusations of betrayal from those who opposed the territorial concessions outlined in the accords.

Role of Incitement: From Rhetoric to Violence:

A toxic undercurrent of incitement and hostile rhetoric permeated the political discourse. Extremist elements within Israeli society vehemently opposed Rabin's peacemaking efforts. Inflammatory speeches, posters depicting Rabin in Nazi uniform, and chants labeling him a traitor contributed to a charged atmosphere. This environment would ultimately provide a breeding ground for violence.

Yigal Amir: The Assassin Within:

Yigal Amir, a right-wing Jewish extremist, emerged as the assassin who shattered the dream of peace. Amir's motivations were rooted in ideological opposition to the Oslo

Accords, fueled by religious and nationalist fervor. His belief that Rabin's concessions endangered Jewish land and security led him to commit the unthinkable act of assassinating the sitting Prime Minister.

The Night of the Assassination: A Nation in Shock:

On the fateful night of November 4, 1995, Rabin attended a peace rally in Tel Aviv's Kings of Israel Square. As he left the stage, Yigal Amir approached and fired three shots at close range. The bullets struck Rabin in the back, inflicting fatal injuries. The nation, which had been cautiously optimistic about the prospects of peace, was plunged into shock and grief.

Immediate Aftermath: Mourning and Outpouring of Grief:

Rabin's assassination triggered an immediate outpouring of grief and disbelief. Israelis from all walks of life gathered to mourn the loss of a leader who had become synonymous with the pursuit of peace. The global community, too, expressed condolences and solidarity, recognizing the profound implications of Rabin's death for the fragile Middle East peace process.

Impact on the Peace Process: Unraveling Hope:

The assassination of Yitzhak Rabin dealt a severe blow to the optimism surrounding the Oslo Accords. Rabin's successor, Shimon Peres, attempted to carry the torch of peace, but the political dynamics had shifted. The assassination created an atmosphere of mistrust and skepticism, undermining the momentum toward a comprehensive peace agreement.

Shift in Political Landscape: Benjamin Netanyahu's Ascendance:

With Rabin's death, the political landscape in Israel underwent a transformation. Benjamin Netanyahu, a vocal critic of the Oslo Accords, assumed leadership. His government took a more cautious approach to the peace process, advocating for a slower pace of negotiations and expressing concerns about the security implications of ceding territory.

Impact on Palestinian Leadership: Navigating Uncertainty:

The assassination also had repercussions on the Palestinian side. Yasser Arafat, who had engaged in peace talks with Rabin, now faced a more hesitant Israeli leadership. The dynamics of the peace process were altered, and the uncertainties introduced by Rabin's assassination added complexity to the already challenging negotiations.

Legacy of Rabin's Assassination: Lessons and Reflections:

The legacy of Yitzhak Rabin's assassination extends beyond the immediate aftermath. It prompts reflection on the fragile nature of the pursuit of peace in a region rife with historical grievances and deep-seated tensions. Rabin's vision of a secure Israel living side by side with a viable Palestinian state endured, but the journey toward that vision became even more treacherous.

Impact on Israeli Society: Reckoning with Extremism:

Rabin's assassination prompted Israeli society to reckon with the presence of extremism within its midst. The act of violence committed by a fellow citizen against a sitting Prime Minister underscored the need for introspection and a collective examination of the forces that could jeopardize the democratic foundations of the state.

Conclusion: A Nation Forever Changed:

The assassination of Yitzhak Rabin stands as a defining moment in the history of Israel and the Israeli-Palestinian conflict. It represents a tragedy not only for the loss of a leader but for the derailment of a peace process that held the promise of a different future. Rabin's death echoes through the years, a stark reminder of the challenges inherent in the pursuit of peace in a region burdened by a complex history and deeply entrenched animosities.

Chapter 4: Roadmap to Peace
The Second Intifada

The outbreak of the Second Intifada in September 2000 marked a tumultuous chapter in the Israeli-Palestinian conflict, disrupting the fragile peace process initiated by the Oslo Accords. This section explores the causes, unfolding events, and consequences of the Second Intifada, shedding light on the complex dynamics that fueled a period of intensified Palestinian uprising and Israeli military responses.

Backdrop of Unresolved Issues:

As the 1990s drew to a close, the optimism following the Oslo Accords gave way to mounting frustrations. Unresolved core issues, including the status of Jerusalem, the right of return for Palestinian refugees, and the expansion of Israeli settlements, lingered as persistent challenges. The failure of the Camp David Summit in 2000 further heightened tensions, providing a backdrop for the eruption of violence.

Triggers of the Second Intifada:

The immediate catalyst for the Second Intifada was a visit to the Temple Mount in Jerusalem by Israeli opposition leader Ariel Sharon on September 28, 2000. The visit, perceived by Palestinians as provocative, triggered protests and clashes. The subsequent Israeli response to the demonstrations fueled a wave of unrest that quickly escalated into a full-scale uprising.

Wave of Protests and Violence:

The Second Intifada witnessed a surge in popular protests, characterized by widespread demonstrations, stone-throwing, and acts of civil disobedience. These grassroots movements were fueled by a sense of disillusionment with the peace process, frustration over living conditions, and a desire for self-determination. The protests soon escalated into a violent confrontation with Israeli security forces.

Israeli Response: From Policing to Military Operation:

As the intensity of the uprising grew, Israel shifted from a policing approach to a more robust military response. The Israeli Defense Forces (IDF) entered Palestinian territories, implementing curfews, conducting arrests, and engaging in military operations. The use of force by both sides resulted in a cycle of violence that claimed the lives of civilians, soldiers, and militants.

Suicide Bombings and Terrorism:

A notable feature of the Second Intifada was the rise of suicide bombings as a tactic employed by Palestinian militant groups. Organizations such as Hamas and Islamic Jihad carried out numerous attacks targeting Israeli civilians, buses, and public spaces. These acts of terrorism deepened the cycle of violence and contributed to a climate of fear and insecurity on both sides.

Siege of the Church of the Nativity:

One of the high-profile incidents during the Second Intifada was the siege of the Church of the Nativity in Bethlehem in April 2002. Palestinian militants sought refuge in the holy site, leading to a standoff with Israeli forces. The siege drew international attention and raised concerns about the impact of the conflict on religious sites.

International Diplomatic Efforts:

International actors sought to intervene diplomatically to quell the violence. Various initiatives, including the Mitchell Report and the Tenet Plan, aimed at establishing ceasefires and creating conditions for the resumption of negotiations. However, the entrenched positions of both parties, coupled with the ongoing violence, hindered the success of these diplomatic efforts.

Impact on Civilian Populations: Humanitarian Crisis:

The Second Intifada had profound humanitarian consequences, particularly for civilian populations. Both Israelis and Palestinians endured loss, injury, and displacement. The conflict disrupted daily life, strained local economies, and exacerbated existing social and economic challenges. The toll on civilian populations underscored the urgency of finding a resolution to the conflict.

Internal Divisions among Palestinians:

The Second Intifada exposed internal divisions within Palestinian society. While many Palestinians supported the uprising as a legitimate expression of resistance, others questioned the effectiveness of the tactics employed and the impact on the Palestinian cause. These internal divisions complicated efforts to present a unified front in negotiations and diplomacy.

Impact on Israeli Society: Security Concerns and Debates:

Within Israel, the Second Intifada prompted a reassessment of security policies and strategies. The rise of suicide bombings and the targeting of civilian areas heightened concerns about national security. Debates within Israeli society centered on the effectiveness of military responses, the need for negotiation, and the broader implications of the ongoing conflict.

Attempts at Ceasefires and Roadmap for Peace:

Amidst the violence, various attempts were made to broker ceasefires and create conditions for renewed peace efforts. The U.S.-led Quartet on the Middle East proposed the Roadmap for Peace in 2003, outlining a step-by-step plan toward the establishment of an independent Palestinian state alongside a secure Israel. However, implementing the roadmap faced challenges, with both sides struggling to fulfill their respective obligations.

Legacy and Long-Term Impact:

The Second Intifada left a lasting impact on the Israeli-Palestinian conflict. The violence and loss of life deepened mutual distrust, making it increasingly challenging to revive the spirit of cooperation that had briefly flourished during the Oslo Accords. The scars of the Second Intifada lingered as a reminder of the fragility of peace in a region fraught with historical grievances and political complexities.

Conclusion: A Period of Turmoil and Consequence:

The Second Intifada stands as a turbulent and consequential period in the history of the Israeli-Palestinian conflict. What began as a response to perceived provocations and frustrations with the peace process evolved into a protracted period of violence and unrest. Understanding the dynamics of the Second Intifada is crucial for comprehending the multifaceted challenges that have shaped the course of negotiations and efforts toward lasting peace in the region.

The Arab Peace Initiative

In the complex landscape of the Israeli-Palestinian conflict, the Arab Peace Initiative emerged as a significant diplomatic effort to address long-standing tensions and establish a comprehensive resolution. This section explores the origins, key components, and implications of the Arab Peace Initiative, shedding light on its role in the quest for a lasting and equitable peace in the Middle East.

Genesis of the Arab Peace Initiative:

The Arab Peace Initiative, proposed by Saudi Arabia in 2002, marked a historic departure in the approach of Arab states toward Israel. Rooted in a desire to achieve a comprehensive resolution to the Israeli-Palestinian conflict, the initiative aimed to normalize relations between Arab states and Israel in exchange for Israel's withdrawal from occupied territories and the establishment of a Palestinian state.

Key Components of the Arab Peace Initiative:

1. Full Withdrawal from Occupied Territories:

Central to the Arab Peace Initiative is the call for Israel to fully withdraw from the territories occupied during the 1967 Six-Day War. This includes the West Bank, East Jerusalem, and the Golan Heights. The initiative envisions the establishment of a sovereign and viable Palestinian state with East Jerusalem as its capital.

2. Resolution of the Refugee Issue:

The initiative addresses the issue of Palestinian refugees, emphasizing a just and agreed-upon solution in accordance with UN General Assembly Resolution 194. The intent is to find a fair resolution that recognizes the rights of refugees and facilitates their return or compensation.

3. Establishment of a Palestinian State:

A fundamental pillar of the Arab Peace Initiative is the creation of an independent and sovereign Palestinian state within the pre-1967 borders, with East Jerusalem as its capital. This aligns with the vision of a two-state solution, a concept widely endorsed by the international community.

4. Normalization of Relations:

In exchange for Israel's compliance with the aforementioned conditions, the Arab Peace Initiative promises full normalization of relations between Israel and the Arab states. This includes diplomatic recognition, economic cooperation, and the establishment of normal ties, breaking the historical pattern of non-recognition and hostility.

Reception and Endorsements:

The Arab Peace Initiative garnered widespread attention and received both praise and criticism from various quarters. Its endorsement by the Arab League, comprising 22 member states, underscored a collective commitment to seeking a comprehensive and just resolution. The initiative also found support from the broader international community, including the European Union.

Challenges and Criticisms:

While the Arab Peace Initiative represented a significant step towards a comprehensive resolution, it faced challenges and criticisms. Some argued that the conditions set for Israel's compliance were too rigid, while others questioned the feasibility of achieving full normalization in a region marked by deep historical animosities.

Role in Subsequent Diplomacy:

The Arab Peace Initiative has played a prominent role in subsequent diplomatic efforts and peace negotiations. It has been referenced in various international forums and has influenced the discourse around the Israeli-Palestinian conflict. The initiative's principles have been reiterated as a basis for negotiation and a potential roadmap for resolving the longstanding issues at the heart of the conflict.

Impact on Regional Dynamics:

The Arab Peace Initiative has had a broader impact on regional dynamics, influencing the relationships between Arab states and Israel. While the initiative has not yet led to full normalization, it has opened avenues for behind-the-scenes cooperation on certain issues of common interest. The initiative's principles continue to be part of the broader conversation on regional stability and security.

Challenges to Implementation:

Despite its potential, the Arab Peace Initiative faces challenges to full implementation. The intricate and deeply rooted nature of the Israeli-Palestinian conflict, coupled with changing geopolitical dynamics, has created obstacles to progress. Internal divisions among Arab states and shifts in leadership have also influenced the initiative's trajectory.

International Recognition and Support:

The Arab Peace Initiative has garnered international recognition and support as a constructive and principled approach to resolving the Israeli-Palestinian conflict. The United Nations, the European Union, and various individual nations have acknowledged the initiative's potential to serve as a foundation for negotiations and a pathway to lasting peace.

Role in Current Peace Initiatives:

The principles outlined in the Arab Peace Initiative continue to inform current peace initiatives and negotiations. Efforts by the international community, including the United States, to facilitate dialogue between Israel and Arab states often reference the initiative's key components as a framework for addressing core issues.

The Future of the Arab Peace Initiative:

As the Israeli-Palestinian conflict persists, the future of the Arab Peace Initiative remains uncertain. Evolving regional dynamics, changes in leadership, and ongoing geopolitical shifts all contribute to the complex landscape. The initiative, however, stands as a testament to the potential for diplomatic solutions and serves as a reminder of the shared responsibility for fostering lasting peace in the Middle East.

Conclusion: A Vision for Comprehensive Peace:

The Arab Peace Initiative, born out of a commitment to resolving the Israeli-Palestinian conflict, represents a bold vision for comprehensive peace in the Middle East. Its endorsement by the Arab League and recognition by the international community highlight its significance. While challenges persist, the initiative remains a crucial component of diplomatic efforts to address the deep-rooted issues at the heart of the enduring conflict.

Security Barrier and Settlements

The construction of the security barrier and the expansion of Israeli settlements in the West Bank have emerged as contentious issues in the Israeli-Palestinian conflict. This section explores the historical context, motivations, and the impact of these measures on the quest for peace, shedding light on the complexities and controversies that surround them.

Historical Context of Settlements:

The establishment of Israeli settlements in the West Bank dates back to the aftermath of the 1967 Six-Day War. Motivated by historical and religious ties to the land, as well as security considerations, Israel initiated the building of settlements in territory captured during the war. Over the years, these settlements have been a focal point of contention, shaping the demographic and geopolitical landscape of the region.

Expansion of Settlements: Dynamics and Challenges:

The expansion of Israeli settlements has been a persistent source of tension in the Israeli-Palestinian conflict. The construction and growth of settlements, often supported by government policies and incentives, have faced criticism from the international community and been a major point of contention in peace negotiations. This section examines the dynamics behind the expansion of settlements, exploring the motivations, challenges, and the impact on the broader peace process.

Security Barrier: Origins and Rationale:

The construction of the security barrier, also known as the Israeli West Bank barrier or separation barrier, commenced in the early 2000s. The primary stated purpose was to enhance security by preventing the infiltration of Palestinian militants into Israeli territory. This section delves into the origins of the security barrier, the motivations behind its construction, and the evolving discourse surrounding its effectiveness and impact on the lives of Palestinians.

Controversies Surrounding the Security Barrier:

While the security barrier has been positioned as a vital security measure by the Israeli government, it has been met with significant controversy. Critics argue that the barrier, in certain sections, deviates from the internationally recognized 1967 borders and has led to the confiscation of Palestinian land. Additionally, the barrier has raised concerns about the impact on Palestinian communities, including access to resources, freedom of movement, and the viability of a future Palestinian state.

Legal and International Perspectives:

The construction of settlements and the security barrier has prompted legal and diplomatic challenges. International law, including the Fourth Geneva Convention, considers the establishment of settlements in occupied territory to be illegal. The International Court of Justice (ICJ) issued an advisory opinion in 2004, stating that the construction of the security barrier violated international law. This section explores the legal perspectives and the implications for diplomatic efforts to address the broader conflict.

Impact on Palestinian Communities: Humanitarian Concerns:

The expansion of settlements and the construction of the security barrier have had significant humanitarian consequences for Palestinian communities. This includes restrictions on movement, economic hardships, and challenges to accessing basic services. The displacement of Palestinian families due to settlement expansion and the alteration of demographics in certain areas have fueled grievances and intensified animosities.

Security Barrier and Israeli Perspective:

From the Israeli perspective, the security barrier is viewed as a crucial measure for protecting civilian lives and preventing terrorist attacks. The government argues that the barrier has been effective in reducing the number of infiltrations and suicide bombings. This section explores the rationale behind the security barrier from an Israeli security standpoint and the complexities involved in balancing security needs with humanitarian considerations.

Settlements as Obstacles to Two-State Solution:

The growth of settlements has been widely criticized for undermining the feasibility of a two-state solution, a concept endorsed by the international community and various peace initiatives. The establishment and expansion of settlements create physical and political obstacles to the creation of a contiguous and viable Palestinian state. This section examines the role of settlements in shaping the contours of a potential peace agreement.

Challenges to Peace Negotiations: Settlements as Stumbling Blocks:

The issue of settlements has been a recurrent stumbling block in peace negotiations between Israelis and Palestinians. Attempts to reach comprehensive agreements have often faltered over disputes related to the status and future of settlements. This section provides an overview of the challenges posed by settlements to diplomatic efforts, exploring specific instances where negotiations faced deadlock due to settlement-related issues.

International Responses and Calls for Resolution:

The international community has responded to the issues of settlements and the security barrier with varying degrees of condemnation and calls for resolution. Resolutions in international forums, statements from world leaders, and diplomatic initiatives have sought to address the contentious aspects of settlement expansion and the impact of the security barrier on the peace process.

Exploring Alternatives and Compromises:

Efforts to find alternatives and compromises regarding settlements and the security barrier have been explored in diplomatic circles. Proposals for land swaps, compensation, and negotiated agreements have been put forward as potential mechanisms for addressing the challenges posed by settlements while safeguarding Israel's security concerns. This section examines some of these proposals and their reception.

Conclusion: Navigating Complexities for a Sustainable Peace:

The issues of settlements and the security barrier underscore the intricate and multifaceted nature of the Israeli-Palestinian conflict. Balancing security imperatives, humanitarian considerations, and the quest for a just and lasting peace requires careful navigation. As diplomatic efforts continue, addressing the controversies surrounding settlements and the security barrier remains a critical component in the broader pursuit of a comprehensive resolution to the longstanding conflict.

The Gaza Disengagement, a landmark event in the Israeli-Palestinian conflict, marked a significant shift in the dynamics of territorial control and raised crucial questions about the path to peace. This section explores the historical context, motivations, and consequences of the Gaza Disengagement, shedding light on the complexities surrounding this pivotal moment in the quest for a resolution to the enduring conflict.

Historical Background:

The roots of the Gaza Disengagement can be traced back to the aftermath of the Oslo Accords in the 1990s. The accords set the stage for the establishment of the Palestinian Authority (PA) and the division of responsibilities between Israel and the newly formed Palestinian governing body. However, as violence escalated and peace efforts faltered, the situation in Gaza became a focal point for both Israeli and Palestinian leaders.

The Vision of the Disengagement:

Proposed by then-Israeli Prime Minister Ariel Sharon, the Gaza Disengagement plan aimed to address security concerns, demographic challenges, and the stalled peace process. Unveiled in 2004, the plan called for the withdrawal of Israeli settlements from the Gaza Strip and parts of the northern West Bank, effectively dismantling communities that had been established over decades.

Dismantling Israeli Settlements: Challenges and Controversies:

The process of dismantling Israeli settlements in Gaza, known as Gush Katif, and parts of the West Bank proved to be a deeply divisive and emotionally charged undertaking. Thousands of Israeli settlers were uprooted from their homes, leading to scenes of resistance, protests, and, in some cases, forcible eviction. The evacuation of settlements also raised questions about compensation, relocation, and the impact on the settlers' lives.

Military Logistics and Humanitarian Concerns:

The logistical challenges of executing the disengagement were immense. The Israel Defense Forces (IDF) faced the complex task of evacuating settlers while maintaining order and preventing violence. Humanitarian concerns arose regarding the relocation of settlers and the potential impact on both Israeli and Palestinian communities. This section explores the intricacies of the military and logistical aspects of the disengagement.

International Response:

The international community closely monitored the Gaza Disengagement, offering varied responses to this unprecedented move. While some viewed it as a positive step towards restarting the peace process, others expressed concerns about the potential for increased instability and the humanitarian impact on Palestinian residents. The reactions from key international players, including the United States and the European Union, shaped the narrative surrounding the disengagement.

Impact on Israeli Society:

The Gaza Disengagement had profound implications for Israeli society. The dismantling of settlements generated heated debates about the future of Israeli territories, the legitimacy of the disengagement, and the government's role in shaping the country's borders. The event left an indelible mark on Israeli politics, contributing to shifts in public opinion and influencing subsequent approaches to territorial concessions.

Impact on Palestinian Territories: Challenges and Opportunities:

While the Gaza Disengagement represented a significant change in territorial control, it also presented challenges and opportunities for the Palestinians. The handover of control in Gaza raised questions about governance, security, and the potential for economic development. The Palestinian Authority faced the task of asserting authority in the evacuated territories while contending with internal divisions and the ongoing Israeli presence in the West Bank.

Unfolding Events in the Aftermath:

The period following the Gaza Disengagement witnessed a complex interplay of events, shaping the trajectory of Israeli-Palestinian relations. The rise of the militant group Hamas, the challenges faced by the Palestinian Authority, and the continuation of violence in the region all added layers of complexity to the already intricate landscape. This section explores the unfolding events and their impact on the broader peace process.

The Legacy of the Gaza Disengagement:

Reflecting on the Gaza Disengagement, its legacy remains a subject of debate and analysis. Some view it as a missed opportunity for advancing peace, while others see it as a necessary and bold move to reshape the parameters of the conflict. Assessing the lasting impact on Israeli and Palestinian communities, as well as its implications for the broader peace process, requires a nuanced understanding of the complexities involved.

Challenges to the Two-State Solution:

The Gaza Disengagement, while addressing certain territorial aspects, raised questions about the overall viability of the two-state solution. The continued presence of Israeli settlements in the West Bank, the status of East Jerusalem, and the lack of a comprehensive agreement on final borders remain significant hurdles to achieving a sustainable and just resolution.

Lessons Learned and Ongoing Dilemmas:

Examining the Gaza Disengagement provides an opportunity to glean lessons about the complexities of peacemaking in the Israeli-Palestinian context. The disengagement offers insights into the challenges of territorial concessions, the role of domestic politics, and the delicate balance between security concerns and the pursuit of a just and lasting peace.

Conclusion: Navigating Uncertainties in the Pursuit of Peace:

The Gaza Disengagement stands as a pivotal moment in the complex narrative of the Israeli-Palestinian conflict. While it marked a significant shift in territorial control, it also underscored the intricate challenges that persist in the pursuit of a comprehensive and sustainable peace. Understanding the motivations, consequences, and ongoing dilemmas surrounding the Gaza Disengagement is essential for comprehending the broader dynamics shaping the future of the region.

Chapter 5: People-to-People Initiatives and Civil Society

Grassroots Efforts for Peace

In the midst of political complexities and diplomatic challenges in the Israeli-Palestinian conflict, grassroots efforts for peace have emerged as a powerful force, demonstrating that change can emanate from the ground up. This section explores the diverse range of grassroots initiatives undertaken by individuals and communities on both sides, highlighting their significance in fostering understanding, dialogue, and a shared vision for a peaceful future.

The Power of Grassroots Movements:

Grassroots movements play a crucial role in the broader landscape of conflict resolution. By operating at the community level, these initiatives bypass traditional political structures, allowing individuals to connect on a personal and human level. This section examines the inherent power of grassroots movements and their potential to bridge divides, challenge stereotypes, and create spaces for genuine dialogue.

Building Bridges Across Communities:

One of the key objectives of grassroots efforts is to build bridges between Israeli and Palestinian communities.

Initiatives such as joint cultural events, sports exchanges, and collaborative artistic projects aim to create shared spaces where individuals from both sides can interact on a human level. This subtopic explores the various ways in which grassroots movements facilitate cross-community connections and foster relationships beyond political boundaries.

Educational Initiatives for Understanding:

Education is a powerful tool for promoting understanding and dispelling stereotypes. Grassroots educational initiatives focus on bringing together Israeli and Palestinian students to learn about each other's histories, cultures, and narratives. This section delves into the impact of educational programs that emphasize empathy, tolerance, and the importance of shared narratives in creating a foundation for lasting peace.

Track II Diplomacy: Grassroots Initiatives as Catalysts for Change:

Grassroots initiatives often operate in parallel with formal diplomatic processes, contributing to a Track II diplomacy approach. This subtopic explores how these people-to-people efforts serve as catalysts for change by fostering connections, creating a shared narrative, and influencing public opinion. The role of grassroots movements in shaping the broader discourse on the conflict is examined, emphasizing their potential to influence policy and public sentiment.

Youth Engagement: Shaping the Future of Peace:

Engaging young people is a central focus of many grassroots initiatives. Youth, who often bear the brunt of the conflict's impact, are seen as key agents of change. Youth-led projects, dialogue programs, and leadership development initiatives are explored in this section, highlighting how empowering the next generation can contribute to a sustainable and enduring peace.

Women as Agents of Change:

Women, both Israeli and Palestinian, have played pivotal roles in grassroots movements for peace. This subtopic examines the unique contributions of women-led initiatives in building bridges, fostering dialogue, and advocating for peace. It explores the ways in which women's perspectives and voices are essential for creating inclusive and resilient peacebuilding efforts.

Interfaith Dialogue and Shared Spaces:

Interfaith dialogue initiatives seek to find common ground among people of different religious backgrounds. Grassroots movements that create shared spaces for worship, dialogue, and cooperation are examined in this section. The role of religious leaders and communities in promoting tolerance, understanding, and collaboration is explored as an essential component of people-to-people efforts.

Challenges and Resilience: Navigating Obstacles to Peace:

While grassroots initiatives bring hope and promise, they also face numerous challenges. This subtopic explores the obstacles encountered by individuals and organizations working at the grassroots level, including political pressures, societal skepticism, and the ongoing impact of the conflict. It examines the resilience of these initiatives in the face of adversity and their ability to adapt and evolve.

Success Stories and Impact Assessment:

Highlighting success stories is integral to understanding the tangible impact of grassroots efforts. This section showcases specific initiatives that have made a meaningful difference in building connections, changing perceptions, and fostering a sense of shared humanity. It also discusses methodologies for assessing the impact of people-to-people initiatives in the long term.

Global Partnerships and Support:

Grassroots movements often benefit from international partnerships and support. This subtopic explores the role of global organizations, NGOs, and individuals in providing resources, funding, and advocacy for people-to-people initiatives. The importance of a collaborative approach that leverages global networks in advancing grassroots efforts is examined.

Challenges to Sustainability and Scalability:

As grassroots initiatives seek to expand their impact, challenges related to sustainability and scalability come to the forefront. This section discusses the difficulties of maintaining momentum, securing funding, and ensuring the long-term viability of people-to-people efforts. It explores strategies for overcoming these challenges and fostering a sustainable landscape for grassroots peacebuilding.

Conclusion: The Transformative Potential of Grassroots Peacebuilding:

Grassroots efforts for peace have the transformative potential to reshape narratives, challenge entrenched perspectives, and create the conditions for genuine understanding. This section concludes by emphasizing the enduring importance of people-to-people initiatives in the Israeli-Palestinian context, underscoring their role as beacons of hope and agents of change in the pursuit of a just and lasting peace.

In the intricate tapestry of the Israeli-Palestinian conflict, economic cooperation has emerged as a compelling avenue for building bridges and fostering mutual understanding. This section explores the dynamics of joint economic ventures between Israelis and Palestinians, examining how shared economic interests can serve as a catalyst for peace and stability in the region.

Historical Context of Economic Cooperation:

Historically, economic ties between Israelis and Palestinians have faced challenges rooted in the broader political conflict. However, pockets of collaboration have emerged, particularly during periods of relative calm. This subtopic delves into the historical context of economic cooperation, exploring moments of collaboration, joint ventures, and shared economic endeavors.

Economic Interdependence:

The concept of economic interdependence suggests that when economies are intertwined, the interests of each party become linked. This section examines how joint economic ventures between Israelis and Palestinians contribute to a sense of shared destiny, where the prosperity of one side is intricately connected to the well-being of the other. It explores economic partnerships that have sought to create mutual dependencies.

Sectoral Collaborations:

Joint economic ventures span various sectors, including agriculture, technology, manufacturing, and tourism. This subtopic explores specific collaborations within each sector, highlighting success stories and challenges faced. It delves into the potential for economic partnerships to transcend political boundaries and create opportunities for shared growth.

Cross-Border Trade and Commerce:

Trade and commerce form the backbone of economic cooperation, providing a tangible expression of shared interests. This section examines cross-border trade initiatives, exploring how businesses on both sides navigate political challenges to engage in mutually beneficial exchanges. It also addresses the role of international actors in facilitating and supporting cross-border trade.

Impact on Local Economies:

The impact of joint economic ventures extends beyond the business realm to influence local economies on both sides. This subtopic explores how collaborative efforts contribute to job creation, economic development, and improved living standards for communities in Israel and the

Palestinian territories. It also examines challenges and opportunities for sustainable economic growth.

Governmental and Non-Governmental Initiatives:

Both governmental and non-governmental entities play crucial roles in promoting and facilitating joint economic ventures. This section explores initiatives led by governments, international organizations, and grassroots organizations that aim to create an enabling environment for economic cooperation. It discusses policy frameworks, incentives, and support mechanisms that encourage collaboration.

Innovation and Technology Partnerships:

Innovation and technology collaborations have emerged as particularly promising areas for joint ventures. This subtopic examines partnerships in research and development, technological innovation, and startup ecosystems. It explores how shared technological advancements can contribute to economic growth and foster a culture of innovation on both sides.

Challenges to Economic Cooperation:

Despite the potential for shared economic ventures, numerous challenges persist. Political tensions, security concerns, and the broader geopolitical context create obstacles to sustained economic cooperation. This section explores the challenges faced by joint economic initiatives, including regulatory barriers, access to resources, and issues related to infrastructure and mobility.

Social and Cultural Impact:

Economic cooperation has the potential to extend beyond financial transactions to influence social and cultural dynamics. This subtopic explores how joint economic ventures contribute to cultural exchange, cross-cultural understanding, and the breaking down of stereotypes. It also addresses the role of people-to-people interactions in shaping perceptions and fostering a sense of shared identity.

Environmental Sustainability in Economic Cooperation:

Environmental considerations have gained prominence in recent discussions about joint economic ventures. This section explores how sustainability practices are integrated into collaborative economic initiatives, addressing issues such as resource management, renewable energy projects, and environmental conservation efforts that transcend political boundaries.

Case Studies of Successful Ventures:

Highlighting successful joint economic ventures provides insights into the tangible benefits of collaboration. This subtopic presents case studies of initiatives that have overcome challenges and demonstrated the transformative potential of economic cooperation. It analyzes the factors contributing to success and draws lessons for future endeavors.

Future Prospects and Opportunities:

Looking ahead, the potential for joint economic ventures to contribute to lasting peace and stability remains significant. This section explores future prospects and opportunities, considering the role of emerging industries, changing geopolitical dynamics, and evolving regional partnerships in shaping the landscape of economic cooperation.

Conclusion: Towards a Shared Economic Future:

Joint economic ventures stand as a testament to the possibility of building bridges and fostering cooperation in the midst of a complex political landscape. This section concludes by underscoring the importance of economic collaboration as a force for positive change, contributing to the broader vision of a shared and prosperous future for Israelis and Palestinians alike.

Interfaith Dialogue and Coexistence

In the heart of the Israeli-Palestinian conflict, interfaith dialogue has emerged as a powerful force, transcending religious boundaries to foster understanding, respect, and cooperation. This section explores the intricate tapestry of interfaith initiatives and coexistence efforts, delving into their role in bridging divides and promoting a shared vision for a harmonious future.

Historical Roots of Interfaith Relations:

The historical context of the region is marked by a mosaic of religious traditions, including Judaism, Islam, and Christianity. This subtopic examines the historical roots of interfaith relations, exploring periods of cooperation, coexistence, and shared cultural influences that have shaped the religious landscape of the Holy Land.

Theological Foundations of Interfaith Dialogue:

Interfaith dialogue is grounded in the recognition of shared theological values and the pursuit of common ground among diverse religious traditions. This section explores the theological foundations that underpin interfaith dialogue, examining how religious teachings and scriptures provide a basis for understanding, tolerance, and cooperation.

Interfaith Initiatives for Peace:

Numerous interfaith initiatives have emerged with the explicit goal of promoting peace and reconciliation in the region. This subtopic explores specific projects, programs, and organizations that bring together leaders and practitioners from different faiths to engage in dialogue, bridge divides, and work towards a shared commitment to peace.

Religious Leaders as Agents of Change:

Religious leaders play a pivotal role in shaping attitudes, fostering understanding, and mobilizing communities towards peaceful coexistence. This section examines the contributions of religious leaders from various faiths in promoting interfaith dialogue. It highlights instances where clergy have come together to advocate for peace and condemn violence, fostering a sense of unity.

Shared Sacred Spaces:

The Holy Land is home to sacred sites revered by multiple faiths, creating a unique opportunity for shared sacred spaces. This subtopic explores instances where religious communities collaborate to maintain and protect these shared sites, emphasizing the potential for mutual respect and cooperation in spaces deemed holy by different faith traditions.

Educational Initiatives for Interfaith Understanding:

Education plays a critical role in promoting interfaith understanding among future generations. This section examines educational initiatives that focus on fostering tolerance, empathy, and appreciation for religious diversity. It explores the impact of interfaith education in breaking down stereotypes and building bridges between communities.

Joint Religious Celebrations and Rituals:

Interfaith dialogue is not confined to formal discussions but extends to joint religious celebrations and rituals. This subtopic explores instances where communities come together to celebrate shared religious festivals, conduct joint prayers, and engage in rituals that promote a sense of unity and common purpose.

Challenges to Interfaith Dialogue:

While interfaith initiatives hold promise, they are not without challenges. This section explores obstacles to interfaith dialogue, including historical grievances, political tensions, and differing interpretations of religious narratives. It delves into the complexities of navigating theological differences and addressing deep-seated mistrust.

Interfaith Dialogue in Conflict Zones:

Interfaith dialogue takes on added significance in areas of conflict, where religious identities can become intertwined with political and nationalistic sentiments. This subtopic examines the role of interfaith dialogue in conflict zones, exploring how it can mitigate religious tensions and contribute to broader peacebuilding efforts.

Women in Interfaith Initiatives:

The inclusion of women in interfaith initiatives brings a unique perspective, often emphasizing collaboration, empathy, and community building. This section explores the role of women in interfaith dialogue, highlighting initiatives led by women that have contributed to fostering understanding and cooperation.

International Support for Interfaith Efforts:

Interfaith dialogue receives support from various international organizations, governments, and non-governmental entities. This subtopic examines the role of global actors in promoting and sustaining interfaith initiatives. It explores how international support contributes to the effectiveness and reach of interfaith dialogue efforts.

Success Stories and Transformative Impact:

Highlighting success stories is integral to understanding the transformative impact of interfaith dialogue. This section presents case studies of interfaith initiatives that have demonstrated tangible positive outcomes, whether in building trust, promoting reconciliation, or fostering a sense of shared responsibility for peace.

Future Prospects for Interfaith Coexistence:

Looking ahead, the prospects for interfaith coexistence remain integral to the vision of a peaceful future. This subtopic explores future possibilities and opportunities for interfaith dialogue, considering how evolving dynamics, changing demographics, and shifting geopolitical landscapes may influence the trajectory of interfaith initiatives.

Conclusion: Harmony in Diversity - The Promise of Interfaith Coexistence:

Interfaith dialogue and coexistence efforts embody the promise of harmony in a diverse and divided landscape. This section concludes by emphasizing the enduring importance of interfaith initiatives in the Israeli-Palestinian context, underscoring their role as catalysts for understanding, respect, and a shared commitment to building a future of peaceful coexistence.

Challenges and Setbacks in Civil Society Initiatives

Civil society initiatives, driven by grassroots organizations and individuals, play a crucial role in fostering peace and understanding in the Israeli-Palestinian conflict. However, the path to meaningful change is fraught with challenges and setbacks. This section explores the complexities faced by civil society initiatives, examining the obstacles that impede progress and hinder the transformative potential of these efforts.

Historical Challenges and Context:

To understand the challenges faced by civil society initiatives, it is essential to delve into the historical context of the Israeli-Palestinian conflict. This subtopic explores the deep-rooted historical challenges that have shaped the current landscape, including territorial disputes, historical grievances, and the complex web of political, religious, and cultural dynamics.

Political Obstacles and State Interference:

Civil society initiatives often face resistance and interference from political authorities on both sides. This section explores how state policies, regulations, and political agendas can create obstacles for organizations working towards peace. It delves into instances of state interference, restrictions on civil society activities, and the broader impact of political dynamics on the effectiveness of peacebuilding efforts.

Security Concerns and Humanitarian Crises:

The region's history of conflict has given rise to persistent security concerns, impacting the ability of civil society organizations to operate freely. This subtopic examines the challenges posed by ongoing security issues, including the impact of conflict-related violence, military operations, and the resulting humanitarian crises on the work of civil society in both Israeli and Palestinian territories.

Resource Constraints and Funding Challenges:

Civil society initiatives often grapple with resource constraints, including limited funding, manpower, and organizational capacity. This section explores how these limitations affect the sustainability and reach of peacebuilding efforts. It delves into the complexities of securing funding, navigating donor priorities, and sustaining initiatives in the face of financial challenges.

Polarization and Divisiveness:

The Israeli-Palestinian conflict is marked by deep-seated polarization and divisiveness, which can infiltrate civil society spaces. This subtopic examines how ideological differences, historical narratives, and societal divisions can hinder collaboration and dialogue within civil society. It explores the impact of polarization on the ability to build inclusive and effective peacebuilding initiatives.

Media Influence and Public Perception:

Media plays a significant role in shaping public perception and influencing attitudes towards peace initiatives. This section explores how media coverage, both local and international, can impact the success or failure of civil society initiatives. It delves into the challenges posed by biased reporting, sensationalism, and the role of media in perpetuating stereotypes and deepening mistrust.

Interference from Extremist Groups:

Extremist groups, with their vested interests in perpetuating the conflict, can pose significant challenges to civil society initiatives. This subtopic examines instances where extremist ideologies interfere with peacebuilding efforts, including threats, intimidation, and violence against individuals and organizations working towards reconciliation.

Cultural and Linguistic Barriers:

Cultural and linguistic differences between Israeli and Palestinian communities can create barriers to effective communication and collaboration. This section explores how these barriers impact the work of civil society initiatives, hindering efforts to bridge divides, build trust, and create meaningful connections between communities with distinct cultural and linguistic identities.

Psychological Trauma and Mental Health Challenges:

The enduring conflict has left a legacy of psychological trauma and mental health challenges for individuals and communities. This subtopic explores how the pervasive impact of trauma can impede the effectiveness of civil society initiatives. It examines the challenges of addressing mental health needs, fostering resilience, and creating spaces for healing within the context of peacebuilding.

International Mediation and Diplomatic Challenges:

Civil society initiatives often seek international support and mediation to amplify their impact. This section explores how diplomatic challenges, geopolitical shifts, and international dynamics can influence the success or failure of civil society efforts. It delves into the complexities of navigating global politics and engaging with international actors in the pursuit of peace.

Intra-Organizational Challenges and Coordination Issues:

Within civil society organizations themselves, internal challenges can arise, affecting their ability to coordinate and implement initiatives effectively. This subtopic explores issues related to organizational structure, leadership dynamics, and coordination between different groups. It examines how these intra-organizational challenges impact the overall effectiveness of peacebuilding efforts.

Learning from Setbacks: Lessons and Adaptations:

Despite the myriad challenges, setbacks can provide valuable lessons for civil society initiatives. This section explores examples where setbacks have led to adaptations, innovations, and a reevaluation of strategies. It highlights the resilience of civil society actors in the face of adversity and examines how learning from setbacks can contribute to the evolution and improvement of peacebuilding approaches.

Conclusion: Overcoming Adversity for a Sustainable Peace:

In the face of formidable challenges, civil society initiatives remain essential agents of change in the Israeli-Palestinian conflict. This section concludes by emphasizing the need for resilience, adaptability, and a collective commitment to overcome obstacles. It underscores the enduring importance of civil society efforts in paving the way for a sustainable and just peace in the region.

Chapter 6: Ongoing Challenges and Regional Dynamics

The Role of International Mediation

International mediation has long been a pivotal element in the quest for resolution in the Israeli-Palestinian conflict. This section delves into the intricate role played by international actors in mediating negotiations, facilitating dialogues, and working towards finding common ground amidst the complexities of the region.

Historical Context of International Mediation:

Understanding the evolution of international mediation in the Israeli-Palestinian conflict requires examining its historical context. This subtopic traces the roots of international involvement, from the early post-World War II period to the present day, highlighting key moments, initiatives, and the changing dynamics of global geopolitics in shaping mediation efforts.

The United Nations and Resolutions:

The United Nations (UN) has been a central figure in international mediation, issuing resolutions and recommendations aimed at addressing the conflict. This section explores the historical involvement of the UN, examining the impact of resolutions such as UN General Assembly Resolution 181 and UN Security Council

Resolution 242. It analyzes the challenges and successes associated with the UN's role in mediating the conflict.

Quartet and Multilateral Diplomacy:

The Quartet on the Middle East, comprising the United States, the European Union, the United Nations, and Russia, represents a unique multilateral approach to international mediation. This subtopic delves into the formation, functions, and effectiveness of the Quartet, assessing its role in promoting dialogue, peace, and a two-state solution.

Bilateral vs. Multilateral Approaches:

International mediation in the Israeli-Palestinian conflict has witnessed both bilateral and multilateral approaches. This section examines the advantages and challenges associated with each approach, exploring how different international actors have engaged in mediation efforts either individually or collectively.

The Oslo Accords and International Mediation:

The Oslo Accords marked a significant turning point in the peace process, and international mediators played a crucial role in facilitating these negotiations. This subtopic analyzes the contributions of international actors in the Oslo Accords, focusing on the roles of Norway, the United States, and other intermediaries in bringing the parties to the negotiating table.

The Role of the United States:

The United States has been a prominent player in international mediation efforts, employing its diplomatic influence and resources. This section explores the historical involvement of the U.S. in mediating the conflict, from the Camp David Accords to various peace initiatives. It assesses the impact of U.S. mediation and the challenges associated with maintaining a neutral stance.

European Union's Diplomatic Engagement:

The European Union (EU) has emerged as a key diplomatic player in the peace process. This subtopic examines the EU's role in international mediation, focusing on diplomatic initiatives, aid programs, and political engagement aimed at promoting peace and stability in the region.

Regional and Arab Mediation Initiatives:

Regional actors, particularly Arab states, have also engaged in mediation efforts to address the Israeli-Palestinian conflict. This section explores the role of regional and Arab mediators, such as Egypt and Jordan, in facilitating dialogue and peace negotiations. It assesses the challenges and opportunities associated with regional mediation initiatives.

The Impact of Changing Administrations:

The role of international mediators is influenced by the political dynamics of individual states. This subtopic analyzes how changes in the administrations of key players, such as the United States, impact the trajectory of international mediation efforts. It explores the challenges of maintaining continuity and effectiveness in the face of shifting political landscapes.

The Quartet and the Roadmap to Peace:

The Quartet's Roadmap to Peace represents a comprehensive plan for resolving the Israeli-Palestinian conflict. This section explores the inception, objectives, and challenges of the Roadmap, assessing the role of the Quartet in its implementation and the broader impact on the peace process.

Challenges to International Mediation:

Despite international efforts, numerous challenges persist in the mediation process. This subtopic examines the obstacles faced by international mediators, including political stalemates, shifting priorities, and the complex web of historical grievances. It assesses how these challenges impact the efficacy of mediation efforts.

The Influence of Global Geopolitical Shifts:

Global geopolitical shifts have a direct bearing on international mediation efforts. This section explores the impact of changing geopolitical dynamics, including shifts in alliances, rising regional powers, and evolving global priorities, on the ability of international actors to mediate effectively.

The Role of Non-Governmental Organizations (NGOs):

Non-governmental organizations (NGOs) often play a complementary role in international mediation efforts. This subtopic examines how NGOs contribute to peacebuilding, track progress, and advocate for specific issues. It assesses the challenges and opportunities associated with the involvement of NGOs in the mediation process.

Evaluating the Effectiveness of International Mediation:

Effectiveness is a critical measure of international mediation. This section evaluates the overall impact of international mediation efforts in the Israeli-Palestinian conflict, considering factors such as progress in peace talks, implementation of agreements, and the establishment of conditions conducive to lasting peace.

Learning from Past Mediation Efforts: Lessons for the Future:

Past mediation efforts provide valuable lessons for shaping future approaches. This subtopic explores how the experiences of international mediators in the Israeli-Palestinian conflict can inform future strategies, policies, and engagements. It assesses the importance of learning from both successes and failures in the pursuit of sustainable peace.

Conclusion: Navigating the Path Ahead for International Mediation:

As the Israeli-Palestinian conflict continues, international mediation remains a critical tool in the pursuit of a peaceful resolution. This section concludes by emphasizing the ongoing importance of international involvement, highlighting the need for adaptability, collaboration, and sustained efforts to navigate the complexities of the region and contribute to a just and lasting peace.

Changing Regional Alliances

The Israeli-Palestinian conflict exists within a broader regional context marked by complex and ever-changing alliances. This section explores the dynamics of regional alliances and their impact on the trajectory of the conflict. As geopolitical landscapes evolve, understanding the role of neighboring states and regional powers is crucial in comprehending the ongoing challenges and opportunities for peace.

Historical Context of Regional Alliances:

To understand the present state of regional alliances, it is essential to delve into their historical roots. This subtopic explores the early alliances and alignments in the region, tracing the geopolitical shifts that have shaped the dynamics of the Israeli-Palestinian conflict. Historical events, such as the Arab-Israeli wars, set the stage for evolving regional relationships.

Arab League and Collective Approaches:

The Arab League has historically played a significant role in shaping regional responses to the Israeli-Palestinian conflict. This section examines the collective approaches taken by Arab states within the Arab League, exploring diplomatic initiatives, joint statements, and coordinated efforts aimed at addressing the conflict. It assesses the impact of these collective actions on the regional dynamics.

Evolving Alliances in the Arab World:

The Arab world has witnessed shifts in alliances and partnerships over the years. This subtopic analyzes how the geopolitical landscape of the Middle East has evolved, including changes in alliances among Arab states. It explores the factors influencing these shifts, such as geopolitical interests, regional rivalries, and the emergence of new power dynamics.

Normalization Agreements and Diplomatic Shifts:

Recent years have seen significant diplomatic shifts, including normalization agreements between Israel and certain Arab states. This section delves into the motivations behind these normalization agreements, exploring the diplomatic, economic, and geopolitical considerations that have led to changes in regional alliances. It assesses the impact of these agreements on the broader peace process.

Iran's Role and Regional Dynamics:

Iran's influence in the region has been a key factor in shaping regional alliances. This subtopic examines Iran's role in the Israeli-Palestinian conflict, exploring its relationships with various actors in the region. It assesses how Iran's geopolitical aspirations, regional interventions, and alliances with non-state actors impact the broader dynamics of the conflict.

Turkey's Involvement and Regional Impact:

Turkey has emerged as a dynamic player in the region, influencing the Israeli-Palestinian conflict through its diplomatic engagements and regional interventions. This section analyzes Turkey's involvement, exploring its relationships with both Israeli and Palestinian authorities, as well as its broader impact on regional dynamics.

The Role of Non-Arab Muslim Countries:

Beyond the Arab world, non-Arab Muslim countries have also played a role in the Israeli-Palestinian conflict. This subtopic examines the involvement of countries like Turkey, Iran, and others, exploring how their geopolitical interests, religious affiliations, and regional strategies contribute to the complex web of regional alliances.

The Impact of Global Power Dynamics:

Global power dynamics, particularly the involvement of major powers outside the region, have a profound impact on the Israeli-Palestinian conflict. This section explores the role of global powers such as the United States, Russia, and China in shaping regional alliances. It assesses how these external influences contribute to the complexities of the conflict.

Security Alliances and Military Dynamics:

Security alliances and military dynamics are integral components of regional geopolitics. This subtopic examines how security agreements, arms deals, and military interventions influence the Israeli-Palestinian conflict. It assesses the role of regional powers in shaping military strategies and security considerations related to the conflict.

Impact of Refugee Crises and Humanitarian Concerns:

Refugee crises and humanitarian concerns stemming from the conflict have regional implications. This section explores how the displacement of Palestinian refugees and humanitarian challenges influence regional alliances. It assesses the responses of neighboring states and regional actors to these ongoing humanitarian crises.

Resource and Economic Alliances:

Economic considerations and resource alliances play a role in shaping regional dynamics. This subtopic examines how economic interests, trade relationships, and resource allocations impact regional alliances in the context of the Israeli-Palestinian conflict. It explores the role of economic cooperation and competition in influencing political alignments.

Media and Public Opinion in Regional Alliances:

Media and public opinion shape perceptions and influence regional alliances. This section explores how media narratives and public sentiment within regional countries impact their positions on the Israeli-Palestinian conflict. It assesses the role of public discourse in shaping diplomatic approaches and regional alignments.

Strategic Implications of Changing Alliances:

The changing landscape of regional alliances has strategic implications for the Israeli-Palestinian conflict. This subtopic analyzes how shifts in alliances influence diplomatic strategies, negotiation dynamics, and the overall pursuit of peace. It explores the strategic considerations of key regional players in the context of evolving alliances.

Challenges to Regional Alliances:

Despite evolving alliances, numerous challenges persist in regional cooperation. This section examines the obstacles and tensions that hinder effective regional alliances in addressing the Israeli-Palestinian conflict. It explores issues such as historical grievances, territorial disputes, and conflicting geopolitical interests that impact regional collaboration.

Opportunities for Regional Cooperation and Peace:

Amidst challenges, there are opportunities for regional cooperation in advancing peace. This subtopic explores potential areas of collaboration, joint initiatives, and diplomatic strategies that could contribute to regional stability and the resolution of the Israeli-Palestinian conflict. It assesses the role of regional actors in seizing these opportunities.

Conclusion: Navigating the Complexities of Regional Alliances for Peace:

Regional alliances play a pivotal role in the ongoing Israeli-Palestinian conflict, reflecting the intricate geopolitical tapestry of the Middle East. This section concludes by emphasizing the dynamic nature of regional alliances, acknowledging the challenges, and highlighting the potential for constructive engagement by regional actors in shaping a path towards lasting peace.

The Rise of Extremism

The Israeli-Palestinian conflict is not only marked by geopolitical complexities but also by the rising tide of extremism, which adds an additional layer of challenge to the pursuit of peace. This section explores the multifaceted aspects of extremism within the context of the conflict, unraveling its historical roots, ideological underpinnings, and the impact on regional dynamics.

Historical Foundations of Extremism:

To comprehend the rise of extremism, it is essential to trace its historical foundations. This subtopic delves into the early roots of extremist ideologies within both Israeli and Palestinian societies, exploring how historical events, territorial disputes, and nationalistic fervor contributed to the emergence of radicalized elements.

Ideological Strands of Extremism:

Extremism in the Israeli-Palestinian conflict is driven by a complex web of ideological strands. This section analyzes the diverse ideological underpinnings of extremist groups, whether rooted in religious fervor, nationalist aspirations, or a combination of both. It explores how these ideologies fuel radicalization and hinder the prospects for peace.

Impact of Extremism on Palestinian Society:

Extremism has left an indelible mark on Palestinian society. This subtopic examines the impact of extremist ideologies on various facets of Palestinian life, including politics, education, and social structures. It assesses how radicalization influences public opinion, shapes political discourse, and contributes to internal divisions within Palestinian communities.

Extremist Movements within Israel:

Extremist movements are not exclusive to one side of the conflict. This section explores the existence of extremist ideologies within Israeli society, investigating how fringe groups with radical agendas impact the domestic political landscape, contribute to tensions, and pose challenges to the pursuit of a peaceful resolution.

The Role of Religion in Extremist Narratives:

Religion often becomes a focal point for extremist narratives, with both Islam and Judaism invoked to justify radical actions. This subtopic explores how religious elements are woven into extremist ideologies, shaping the narratives of groups on both sides of the conflict. It assesses the role of religious leaders and institutions in either fostering or countering extremism.

External Influences and State-Sponsored Extremism:

Extremist ideologies can be fueled by external influences and, in some cases, even sponsored by states. This section examines how regional and international actors may play a role in supporting extremist groups, either directly or indirectly. It explores the impact of external support on the strength and resilience of extremist movements.

The Nexus Between Extremism and Terrorism:

Extremism often finds expression through acts of terrorism. This subtopic explores the nexus between extremist ideologies and terrorism within the Israeli-Palestinian conflict. It analyzes the tactics employed by extremist groups, their motivations, and the challenges posed to regional security by acts of terrorism.

Social Media and Online Radicalization:

In the digital age, social media platforms have become powerful tools for the spread of extremist ideologies. This section examines the role of social media in facilitating online radicalization, recruiting new members, and amplifying extremist narratives. It assesses the challenges of countering online radicalization in the context of the Israeli-Palestinian conflict.

Impact on Peace Negotiations and Diplomacy:

Extremism exerts a significant influence on the prospects for peace negotiations and diplomatic initiatives.

This subtopic explores how the presence of extremist elements complicates the negotiation process, undermines trust-building efforts, and creates obstacles to the success of peace talks. It assesses the strategies employed to address extremism within diplomatic frameworks.

Human Rights Violations and Extremist Actions:

Extremist actions often result in human rights violations, impacting individuals and communities on both sides of the conflict. This section examines instances where extremist groups engage in acts that violate human rights, exploring the consequences for affected populations and the challenges of holding perpetrators accountable.

Counterterrorism Measures and Civil Liberties:

Governments often respond to extremism with counterterrorism measures, but these measures can have implications for civil liberties. This subtopic explores the delicate balance between ensuring national security and safeguarding individual rights. It assesses the challenges of implementing effective counterterrorism strategies without compromising essential democratic principles.

Extremism in Refugee Camps and Displaced Communities:

Refugee camps and displaced communities become breeding grounds for extremism, with residents facing dire conditions and limited opportunities. This section examines how extremist ideologies take root in these environments, exploring the challenges of preventing radicalization and addressing the unique vulnerabilities of displaced populations.

Impact on Regional Stability and Security:

The rise of extremism has broader implications for regional stability and security. This subtopic analyzes how extremist elements contribute to regional tensions, create security challenges for neighboring states, and influence the overall geopolitical landscape. It assesses the efforts to address extremism as part of broader regional security strategies.

International Cooperation in Countering Extremism:

Given the transnational nature of extremism, international cooperation is crucial in countering radicalization and terrorism. This section explores collaborative efforts among nations, international organizations, and civil society to address extremism in the context of the Israeli-Palestinian conflict. It assesses the effectiveness of these cooperative endeavors.

Education and De-radicalization Programs:

Countering extremism requires proactive measures, including education and de-radicalization programs. This subtopic examines initiatives aimed at preventing radicalization and rehabilitating individuals who have been influenced by extremist ideologies. It assesses the role of education in fostering tolerance, understanding, and countering the appeal of radicalization.

Challenges to Countering Extremism:

Countering extremism is fraught with challenges, ranging from the complexities of ideological narratives to the difficulties of implementing effective policies. This section explores the obstacles faced by governments, civil society, and international actors in their efforts to counter extremism and promote peace.

Future Scenarios and Mitigating Extremist Threats:

This subtopic explores potential future scenarios regarding the trajectory of extremism in the Israeli-Palestinian conflict. It assesses the risks associated with ongoing radicalization and terrorism, highlighting strategies for mitigating extremist threats and fostering conditions conducive to lasting peace.

Conclusion: Navigating the Perils of Extremism in the Pursuit of Peace:

As the Israeli-Palestinian conflict grapples with the rise of extremism, this section concludes by emphasizing the intricate challenges posed by radicalization. It underscores the importance of addressing extremism as an integral part of the broader peace process, recognizing the need for comprehensive strategies that go beyond traditional diplomatic approaches.

The Israeli-Palestinian conflict exists within a geopolitical landscape that is subject to constant shifts and transformations. This section explores the profound impacts of geopolitical changes on the dynamics of the conflict, examining how alterations in regional and global politics influence the prospects for peace and shape the overall trajectory of the Israeli-Palestinian relationship.

Historical Context of Geopolitical Shifts:

Understanding the contemporary impacts of geopolitical shifts requires an exploration of their historical roots. This subtopic delves into key historical events that have shaped the geopolitical context of the Israeli-Palestinian conflict, examining how changes in alliances, global power structures, and regional dynamics have contributed to the complex geopolitical environment.

The Cold War and its Legacy:

The Cold War era left an enduring imprint on the Middle East, influencing the geopolitical dynamics of the Israeli-Palestinian conflict. This section explores how Cold War rivalries and superpower interventions contributed to regional tensions, alliances, and the overall geopolitical framework. It assesses the lasting legacy of the Cold War on the conflict.

Post-Cold War Unipolarity:

The post-Cold War era ushered in a period of unipolarity dominated by the United States. This subtopic examines how the shift from bipolarity to unipolarity impacted the Israeli-Palestinian conflict, influencing diplomatic initiatives, regional alignments, and the role of global powers in mediating the peace process.

Emergence of New Regional Players:

Recent years have witnessed the emergence of new regional players with growing influence in the Middle East. This section analyzes the impact of the rise of nations such as Turkey, Iran, and others on the geopolitical dynamics of the Israeli-Palestinian conflict. It explores how these new actors shape alliances, mediate disputes, and impact regional stability.

Changing Alliances in the Arab World:

Alliances within the Arab world have undergone significant transformations. This subtopic examines how changing alliances among Arab states impact the Israeli-Palestinian conflict. It explores the dynamics of Arab solidarity, the normalization of relations with Israel, and the challenges posed by shifting allegiances within the Arab League.

Global Powers and Their Influence:

Global powers play a crucial role in shaping the geopolitical landscape of the Israeli-Palestinian conflict. This section explores the influence of major powers, including the United States, Russia, China, and the European Union, on the conflict's dynamics. It assesses how the priorities and policies of these global actors impact regional stability.

The Influence of Non-State Actors:

Non-state actors, including transnational organizations and militant groups, exert influence on the Israeli-Palestinian conflict. This subtopic examines the role of non-state actors in shaping the geopolitical landscape, exploring how their actions contribute to regional tensions, conflict escalation, and challenges to peacebuilding efforts.

Impact of Regional Conflicts:

Regional conflicts have a ripple effect on the Israeli-Palestinian conflict. This section analyzes how conflicts in neighboring regions, such as Syria, Lebanon, and Iraq, influence the dynamics of the Israeli-Palestinian relationship. It explores the spillover effects, refugee crises, and the broader impact of regional instability on the pursuit of peace.

Resource Politics and Economic Shifts:

The control and distribution of resources play a significant role in geopolitical dynamics. This subtopic examines how resource politics and economic shifts influence the Israeli-Palestinian conflict. It explores issues such as water rights, energy resources, and economic cooperation, assessing their impact on regional stability and peace prospects.

The Role of International Organizations:

International organizations contribute to shaping the geopolitical landscape of the Israeli-Palestinian conflict. This section explores the role of organizations such as the United Nations, the Arab League, and others in influencing diplomatic initiatives, mediating disputes, and advocating for the rights of Palestinians. It assesses the effectiveness of international organizations in addressing the conflict.

Geopolitical Shifts and Security Dynamics:

Changes in geopolitical alignments have direct implications for security dynamics in the region. This subtopic examines how shifts in alliances and global power structures impact the security considerations of the Israeli and Palestinian authorities. It assesses the challenges posed by evolving security dynamics and the strategies employed to address them.

The Impact of the Abraham Accords:

The Abraham Accords represent a recent and significant geopolitical development in the Middle East. This section analyzes the impact of the normalization agreements between Israel and several Arab states on the Israeli-Palestinian conflict. It explores how the Abraham Accords reshape regional alliances, influence public opinion, and impact the broader pursuit of peace.

Regional Power Competition and Rivalries:

Competition and rivalries among regional powers shape the geopolitical landscape of the Middle East. This subtopic examines how power struggles among nations, such as Iran and Saudi Arabia, impact the Israeli-Palestinian conflict. It explores the proxy dynamics, regional interventions, and the broader consequences of power competition on the pursuit of peace.

Climate Change and Environmental Dynamics:

Climate change and environmental factors contribute to the geopolitical challenges in the region. This section explores the impact of climate-related issues, such as water scarcity and environmental degradation, on the Israeli-Palestinian conflict. It assesses how these challenges exacerbate existing tensions and influence regional stability.

The Influence of Public Opinion:

Public opinion plays a role in shaping the geopolitical landscape. This subtopic examines how the sentiments of populations within Israel, Palestine, and the broader Middle

East impact geopolitical shifts. It explores the role of media, social movements, and public discourse in influencing regional dynamics and the pursuit of peace.

Challenges to Diplomatic Initiatives:

Geopolitical shifts pose challenges to diplomatic initiatives aimed at resolving the conflict. This section analyzes how changes in alliances, power structures, and regional dynamics create obstacles to successful peace negotiations. It explores the difficulties faced by diplomats in navigating the complexities of the evolving geopolitical landscape.

Opportunities for Diplomatic Engagement:

Amidst challenges, geopolitical shifts also create opportunities for diplomatic engagement. This subtopic explores how changes in alliances and global power dynamics open new avenues for diplomatic initiatives. It assesses the potential for leveraging geopolitical shifts to build consensus, foster dialogue, and advance the prospects for a lasting peace.

Conclusion: Adapting to Geopolitical Realities in the Pursuit of Peace:

As the Israeli-Palestinian conflict navigates the ever-changing geopolitical landscape, this section concludes by emphasizing the importance of adapting to geopolitical realities. It underscores the need for nuanced diplomacy, strategic alliances, and a comprehensive understanding of the impact of geopolitical shifts on the pursuit of a just and enduring peace.

Chapter 7: Human Stories and Resilience
Personal Narratives of Conflict

In the vast tapestry of the Israeli-Palestinian conflict, individual stories emerge as poignant threads, weaving a narrative that transcends the geopolitical complexities. This section delves into the personal narratives of those directly affected by the conflict, providing a human dimension to the struggle and offering insights into the profound impact it has on individuals and communities.

The Power of Personal Stories:

Personal narratives have the power to humanize conflicts, offering a unique lens through which to understand the experiences of those living in the midst of turmoil. This subtopic explores the significance of personal stories in shedding light on the multifaceted nature of the Israeli-Palestinian conflict. It emphasizes how individual voices contribute to a more empathetic and nuanced understanding of the challenges faced by people on both sides.

Voices from the Ground: Palestinian Perspectives:

This section presents personal narratives from Palestinians who have directly experienced the conflict. Through firsthand accounts, it explores the lived realities of individuals living in the West Bank, Gaza Strip, East Jerusalem, and beyond. These narratives offer insights into the daily challenges, aspirations, and resilience of Palestinians amidst the ongoing struggle.

Life in Conflict Zones:

Personal stories from conflict zones provide a glimpse into the everyday lives of individuals navigating the complexities of occupation, checkpoints, and military incursions. This subtopic delves into the experiences of Palestinians living in areas directly affected by the conflict, highlighting the impact of political instability on their homes, families, and communities.

Stories of Displacement and Refugees:

Displacement is a harsh reality for many Palestinians, whether due to historical events or more recent conflicts. This section shares narratives of individuals who have been displaced, exploring the emotional toll and practical challenges of rebuilding lives in new environments. It also addresses the enduring connection to ancestral lands and the dreams of return.

Family Narratives and Generational Perspectives:

The conflict's impact is intergenerational, shaping the narratives of families across decades. This subtopic explores family stories, tracing the experiences of individuals and their ancestors. It examines how the conflict's enduring presence influences the perspectives and aspirations of different generations within Palestinian families.

Dreams and Aspirations Amidst Adversity:

Personal narratives often reveal the dreams and aspirations that persist even in the face of adversity. This section explores the hopes of Palestinians for a better future, emphasizing the resilience that fuels their determination to build a life of dignity, security, and opportunity despite the challenges posed by the conflict.

Israeli Narratives: Perspectives from Within:

To provide a comprehensive view, this part of the chapter incorporates personal narratives from Israelis who have been directly impacted by the conflict. These narratives offer insights into the diverse experiences of Jewish and Arab Israelis, exploring the complexities of coexistence, shared identities, and the challenges of living in a region marked by historical tensions.

Voices of Israeli Soldiers and Their Families:

The narratives of Israeli soldiers and their families add another layer to the personal stories within the conflict. This subtopic examines the experiences of those who have served in the Israeli military, delving into the challenges they face and the impact of military service on individuals and their families.

Living with Security Concerns:

Security concerns are a constant presence in the lives of Israelis, shaping their daily routines and decisions. This section explores the narratives of individuals living with the constant awareness of security threats, examining the psychological and emotional toll of navigating life in a region marked by conflict.

Dialogues Across Divides: Joint Narratives of Coexistence:

Amidst the narratives of conflict, there are stories of individuals and groups working towards coexistence. This subtopic highlights joint narratives that bridge divides between Israelis and Palestinians. It explores initiatives, partnerships, and dialogues that seek to foster understanding, empathy, and shared narratives of hope amidst a challenging backdrop.

Intersectionality and Diverse Identities:

Personal narratives reveal the diversity of identities within both the Palestinian and Israeli communities. This section explores the intersectionality of identities, including those of women, LGBTQ+ individuals, religious minorities, and others. It examines how these intersecting identities shape unique narratives within the broader context of the Israeli-Palestinian conflict.

Artistic Expressions as Narrative:

Art serves as a powerful medium for expressing the complexities of the conflict. This subtopic explores the narratives embedded in various forms of artistic expression, including literature, visual arts, music, and film. It examines how artists use their creations to convey personal stories, challenge stereotypes, and contribute to a richer understanding of the human experiences within the conflict.

The Challenges of Bearing Witness:

Sharing personal narratives comes with its own set of challenges. This section explores the complexities of bearing witness to the stories of others, acknowledging the emotional toll on storytellers and the ethical considerations of amplifying personal narratives in the broader discourse on the conflict.

The Role of Oral History and Memory:

Oral history plays a crucial role in preserving personal narratives across generations. This subtopic delves into the importance of oral history and collective memory in documenting the experiences of individuals affected by the conflict. It explores how storytelling becomes a means of passing down knowledge, fostering resilience, and preserving the cultural fabric of communities.

Narratives of Hope and Resilience:

Amidst the hardships, personal narratives often carry messages of hope and resilience. This section highlights stories of individuals who, despite the challenges, have found ways to build bridges, foster understanding, and contribute to the vision of a peaceful coexistence. It emphasizes the capacity of individuals to shape narratives that inspire positive change.

Conclusion: A Mosaic of Voices in the Struggle for Understanding:

This chapter concludes by reflecting on the rich mosaic of voices that emerges from the personal narratives of the Israeli-Palestinian conflict. It emphasizes the importance of listening to these voices, acknowledging the shared humanity within the struggle, and recognizing the potential for empathy and understanding to pave the way for a more just and peaceful future.

Voices for Peace and Coexistence

In the midst of the Israeli-Palestinian conflict's tumultuous history, voices advocating for peace and coexistence have emerged as beacons of hope. This section explores the narratives of individuals and groups actively working towards a shared future of understanding, cooperation, and reconciliation. Through these stories, it seeks to illuminate the transformative power of dialogue, cooperation, and shared humanity.

The Courage to Advocate for Peace:

Individuals who courageously advocate for peace often stand against prevailing narratives of division. This subtopic examines the stories of peace activists and advocates on both sides of the conflict, exploring the personal motivations, challenges faced, and the impact of their efforts on fostering dialogue and understanding.

Cross-Border Partnerships and Initiatives:

In the pursuit of peace, some voices extend beyond national borders, fostering cross-border partnerships and initiatives. This section delves into narratives of individuals and organizations that transcend geopolitical divides, working collaboratively to build bridges, facilitate dialogue, and promote mutual understanding between Israelis and Palestinians.

Joint Israeli-Palestinian Projects:

Peaceful coexistence is often nurtured through joint projects that bring together individuals from both communities. This subtopic explores narratives of joint Israeli-Palestinian initiatives in various fields such as education, healthcare, arts, and business. It examines how collaboration fosters relationships, breaks down stereotypes, and contributes to the vision of a shared future.

Educators and Peacemakers:

Education plays a pivotal role in shaping future perspectives. This section highlights the narratives of educators and peacemakers who work within schools, universities, and community settings to promote understanding, tolerance, and empathy among young generations. It explores the challenges and successes of educational initiatives focused on peacebuilding.

Interfaith Leaders and Initiatives:

Religious diversity is a significant aspect of the Israeli-Palestinian landscape. This subtopic explores the narratives of interfaith leaders and initiatives that bridge religious divides, fostering dialogue and collaboration between Jewish, Muslim, and Christian communities. It examines how religious leaders contribute to the promotion of peaceful coexistence.

Women as Agents of Peace:

Women often play crucial roles in peacebuilding efforts. This section delves into the narratives of women who actively engage in initiatives that promote peace and reconciliation. It explores the unique perspectives and contributions of women in peacebuilding, addressing the gender-specific challenges and opportunities they encounter.

Youth Movements for Peace:

The younger generation is instrumental in shaping the future of the region. This subtopic explores the narratives of youth movements and initiatives that actively promote peace, dialogue, and cross-cultural understanding. It examines the role of young activists in challenging entrenched narratives and fostering a sense of shared responsibility for a peaceful future.

Former Combatants Working for Peace:

Individuals who have served in armed conflicts often bring unique perspectives to the peacebuilding process. This section explores the narratives of former combatants, both Israeli and Palestinian, who have chosen to work towards reconciliation and peace. It examines the challenges of transitioning from conflict to cooperation and the potential impact of these voices on broader societal attitudes.

Cultural Exchanges and Artistic Collaborations:

Cultural exchanges and artistic collaborations provide alternative platforms for dialogue and understanding. This subtopic explores narratives of individuals and groups engaged in cultural and artistic initiatives that transcend political boundaries. It examines how creative expressions contribute to building connections and fostering a shared cultural identity.

Local Grassroots Movements:

Change often begins at the grassroots level. This section highlights the narratives of local grassroots movements that emerge from within communities to promote peace and coexistence. It examines the strategies employed by these movements to address the unique challenges faced by communities on both sides of the conflict.

Diplomats and Peace Negotiators:

Diplomacy plays a critical role in the pursuit of peace. This subtopic explores the narratives of diplomats and peace negotiators who have been actively engaged in diplomatic efforts to resolve the Israeli-Palestinian conflict. It examines the complexities of negotiating peace agreements, the challenges faced, and the impact of diplomatic initiatives on the broader peace process.

International Support for Peace:

International actors and organizations often play a supportive role in peacebuilding endeavors. This section explores narratives of individuals and organizations from the international community actively engaged in supporting peace initiatives in the Israeli-Palestinian context. It examines the impact of international efforts on local peacebuilding processes.

Challenges and Setbacks in Peace Advocacy:

Despite the noble intentions of those advocating for peace, challenges and setbacks are inevitable. This subtopic explores the narratives of individuals who have faced obstacles, criticism, and even hostility in their pursuit of peace. It examines the resilience of peace advocates in the face of adversity and the strategies employed to overcome challenges.

The Role of Media and Information Sharing:

Media and information sharing platforms play a crucial role in shaping public narratives. This section explores the narratives of individuals and organizations working in media and information dissemination to promote narratives of peace and coexistence. It examines the challenges of countering divisive narratives and fostering constructive dialogue.

Lessons from Successful Peacebuilding Initiatives:

Some peacebuilding initiatives have achieved tangible success. This subtopic examines narratives from initiatives that have effectively contributed to fostering peace and cooperation. It analyzes the key components of successful peacebuilding, drawing lessons that can inform future efforts in the pursuit of lasting reconciliation.

Reflections on Personal Transformation:

Engaging in peace advocacy often involves personal transformation. This section explores narratives of individuals who have undergone personal and ideological transformations in their journey towards advocating for peace. It examines how personal experiences shape perspectives and contribute to a broader shift in societal attitudes.

The Vision for a Shared Future:

Amidst the narratives of peace advocates, there is a common vision for a shared future. This subtopic explores the collective aspirations of those working towards peace and coexistence, envisioning a region where Israelis and Palestinians live side by side in mutual respect, understanding, and cooperation.

Conclusion: Sustaining Hope and Building Bridges:

As this chapter concludes, it reflects on the narratives of those actively working for peace and coexistence in the

Israeli-Palestinian context. It emphasizes the enduring hope embedded in these stories and the transformative power of individuals committed to building bridges across divides. The chapter underscores the importance of sustaining these efforts for a future marked by peace and understanding.

The Resilience of Communities

In the face of prolonged conflict and adversity, communities on both sides of the Israeli-Palestinian divide have demonstrated remarkable resilience. This section explores the collective strength and adaptive capacities of communities as they contend with the multifaceted challenges arising from decades of conflict. Through narratives of resilience, it aims to provide insights into the ways communities endure, rebuild, and sustain hope in the midst of adversity.

Historical Trauma and Collective Memory:

Communities carry the weight of historical trauma, shaping their collective memory and identity. This subtopic delves into how historical events, such as the Nakba and the Six-Day War, have left lasting imprints on the psyche of Palestinian and Israeli communities. It examines how the resilience of communities is intertwined with their ability to navigate and reinterpret historical narratives.

The Impact of Displacement and Refugee Communities:

Displacement is a harsh reality for many Palestinian communities, with generations living in exile. This section explores the narratives of resilience within refugee communities, both in the occupied territories and in the diaspora. It examines how these communities maintain cultural identity, foster solidarity, and navigate the challenges of living in protracted displacement.

Life in Conflict Zones:

Communities situated in conflict zones face unique challenges, from daily security concerns to the disruption of essential services. This subtopic delves into the narratives of communities living in areas directly affected by the conflict, such as the Gaza Strip and the West Bank. It explores the resilience strategies employed by these communities to cope with the constant pressures of conflict.

Surviving Economic Hardship:

Economic instability is a pervasive challenge in the region, impacting the livelihoods of both Israeli and Palestinian communities. This section examines how communities navigate economic hardship, exploring the resilience strategies employed to sustain livelihoods, build economic alternatives, and withstand the impact of political and economic uncertainties.

The Role of Civil Society and Community Organizations:

Civil society and community organizations play a vital role in fostering resilience. This subtopic explores the narratives of grassroots initiatives, NGOs, and community-based organizations actively working to address the needs of vulnerable communities. It examines the ways in which these organizations empower communities, build social capital, and contribute to overall resilience.

Coping with Trauma and Mental Health Challenges:

Prolonged conflict takes a toll on the mental health of individuals and communities. This section delves into narratives of communities coping with trauma, grief, and mental health challenges. It explores the efforts made by communities to address mental health stigma, provide support systems, and build resilience in the face of psychological distress.

The Role of Education in Building Resilience:

Education is a cornerstone for building resilience within communities. This subtopic explores the narratives of educational initiatives and schools that navigate the challenges of providing quality education in the midst of conflict. It examines how education becomes a tool for empowerment, fostering critical thinking, and nurturing the resilience of the younger generation.

Community-Based Peacebuilding Initiatives:

Communities actively engage in peacebuilding initiatives that contribute to their resilience. This section explores narratives of grassroots peacebuilding efforts, intercommunity dialogues, and conflict resolution initiatives. It examines how communities take agency in promoting understanding, reconciliation, and peaceful coexistence from the grassroots level.

Women as Pillars of Resilience:

Women often emerge as pillars of resilience within communities, playing multifaceted roles in navigating challenges and building social cohesion. This subtopic explores the narratives of women who lead and participate in community resilience efforts. It examines how women contribute to the fabric of community life, address gender-specific challenges, and foster resilience.

Youth Engagement and Empowerment:

The younger generation is integral to the resilience of communities. This section delves into narratives of youth engagement and empowerment initiatives that channel the energy and aspirations of young people toward positive change. It explores how youth initiatives contribute to community resilience, bridge generational gaps, and build a sense of collective agency.

Faith and Community:

Religious and spiritual communities provide a source of strength and resilience. This subtopic explores how faith-based organizations and religious communities contribute to resilience, offering support, guidance, and a sense of community belonging. It examines the ways in which faith intersects with the challenges of conflict, providing solace and fostering a sense of purpose.

Adapting to Environmental Challenges:

Communities in the region face environmental challenges exacerbated by the conflict. This section explores the narratives of communities adapting to environmental changes, such as water scarcity and environmental degradation. It examines resilience strategies that integrate sustainable practices, community-led conservation efforts, and address the broader environmental impact of the conflict.

Intercommunal Solidarity and Cooperation:

Resilience often emerges through intercommunal solidarity and cooperation. This subtopic explores narratives of communities that transcend political and religious divides to work together for common goals. It examines instances of shared resources, joint initiatives, and cooperative efforts that foster resilience by building bridges across communities.

The Role of Traditional Practices and Cultural Heritage:

Traditional practices and cultural heritage contribute to the resilience of communities. This section explores how communities draw upon their cultural heritage and traditional practices to sustain social cohesion, transmit collective wisdom, and navigate the challenges of modern conflicts. It examines the adaptive nature of cultural resilience in the face of external pressures.

Navigating Legal Challenges and Human Rights:

Communities grapple with legal challenges and human rights issues that impact their resilience. This subtopic delves into narratives of communities advocating for their rights, navigating legal frameworks, and addressing issues of justice. It examines how legal resilience becomes a tool for communities to assert their rights, seek accountability, and challenge systemic injustices.

Digital Connectivity and Information Networks:

In the digital age, connectivity becomes a key aspect of community resilience. This section explores narratives of communities leveraging digital technologies and information networks to connect, share information, and mobilize resources. It examines how digital resilience enhances community voices, facilitates communication, and provides a platform for collective action.

Challenges and Threats to Community Resilience:

Despite resilience, communities face ongoing challenges and threats. This subtopic explores narratives of communities contending with external pressures, political volatility, and existential threats. It examines the complexities of sustaining resilience in the face of recurrent challenges and identifies the common threads that bind communities together.

Conclusion: The Endurance of Community Bonds in the Face of Adversity:

As this chapter concludes, it reflects on the narratives of resilience within Israeli and Palestinian communities. It underscores the enduring strength of community bonds, the adaptive capacities developed over decades of conflict, and the hope sustained even in the most challenging circumstances. The chapter emphasizes the collective resilience that serves as a foundation for envisioning a future marked by healing, understanding, and sustainable peace.

Women in Peacebuilding

This section illuminates the pivotal role that women play in peacebuilding efforts within the context of the Israeli-Palestinian conflict. Through narratives and stories, it explores the multifaceted contributions of women, examining their unique perspectives, challenges faced, and the transformative impact they have on fostering dialogue, reconciliation, and sustainable peace in the region.

The Role of Women in Conflict Resolution:

Traditionally relegated to the sidelines, women have increasingly stepped into active roles as agents of change in conflict resolution. This subtopic delves into the historical context of women's involvement in conflict resolution, highlighting instances where women have emerged as mediators, negotiators, and advocates for peace within the Israeli-Palestinian conflict.

Challenges Faced by Women in Peacebuilding:

Despite their essential contributions, women in peacebuilding encounter distinct challenges. This section explores the hurdles faced by women, including societal expectations, gender-based violence, and the struggle for representation within peacebuilding processes. It also examines the resilience of women who navigate these challenges, often leveraging adversity to fuel their commitment to peace.

Voices from the Grassroots: Women-led Initiatives:

At the grassroots level, women-led initiatives have played a crucial role in fostering dialogue and understanding. This subtopic delves into narratives of women initiating and leading projects that bring together individuals from diverse backgrounds. It explores how these initiatives contribute to building bridges, dispelling stereotypes, and fostering collaborative efforts for peace.

Women as Mediators and Negotiators:

Women have increasingly taken on roles as mediators and negotiators, bringing a unique perspective to conflict resolution. This section explores narratives of women who have actively engaged in mediating between Israeli and Palestinian communities. It examines the approaches, challenges, and successes of women involved in formal and informal peace negotiations.

Empowering Women Through Education:

Education is a cornerstone for empowerment, and women actively engage in educational initiatives to promote peace. This subtopic examines narratives of women-led educational projects that foster dialogue, critical thinking, and conflict resolution skills among youth. It explores how education becomes a tool for empowerment, equipping the younger generation to contribute to a peaceful future.

Women and Interfaith Dialogue: Bridging Divides:

Interfaith dialogue is a powerful avenue for fostering understanding and cooperation. This section explores the narratives of women engaged in interfaith initiatives, bridging divides between Jewish, Muslim, and Christian communities. It examines how women contribute to the promotion of religious tolerance, mutual respect, and shared values as essential elements of peacebuilding.

Women's Grassroots Activism for Human Rights:

Human rights activism is a critical aspect of peacebuilding, and women often take a lead role in advocating for justice and equality. This subtopic delves into narratives of women at the forefront of grassroots movements that address human rights violations, advocate for the rights of marginalized communities, and challenge systemic injustices within the conflict context.

The Impact of Women's Leadership in Community Resilience:

Women's leadership is instrumental in building community resilience. This section explores narratives of women who have emerged as leaders within their communities, steering resilience efforts, and contributing to the overall well-being of their societies. It examines how women's leadership fosters cohesion, addresses community needs, and sustains hope amidst adversity.

Stories of Women Affected by Conflict:

Women are not only agents of change but also individuals profoundly affected by the conflict. This subtopic shares narratives of women who have experienced the direct impact of the Israeli-Palestinian conflict. It explores their stories of resilience, survival, and their aspirations for a future marked by peace and stability.

Cross-Border Initiatives Led by Women:

Cross-border initiatives led by women have the potential to transcend political divides. This section delves into narratives of women who initiate and participate in projects that foster cooperation and understanding across Israeli and Palestinian borders. It examines how these initiatives contribute to building connections, dispelling stereotypes, and promoting mutual respect.

Women in Diaspora: Sustaining Transnational Peace Efforts:

The diaspora plays a significant role in peacebuilding, and women within diaspora communities contribute to transnational efforts. This subtopic explores narratives of women in the diaspora who actively engage in peacebuilding initiatives, supporting dialogue, and advocating for a just and lasting resolution to the Israeli-Palestinian conflict from afar.

Women as Agents of Social Change:

Women act as catalysts for broader social change. This section explores narratives of women who challenge societal norms, advocate for gender equality, and contribute to reshaping cultural attitudes within their communities. It examines how women's activism extends beyond peacebuilding, influencing broader social dynamics within the Israeli-Palestinian context.

Cultural Challenges and Transformative Narratives:

Cultural norms can present challenges to women's active involvement in peacebuilding. This subtopic explores narratives of women who navigate cultural barriers, challenge stereotypes, and redefine traditional gender roles within the context of conflict. It examines how women's transformative narratives contribute to reshaping societal perceptions and fostering inclusivity.

Building Bridges Through Women's Networks:

Women's networks provide platforms for collaboration and solidarity. This section delves into narratives of women actively engaged in networks that bridge divides, fostering connections between Israeli and

Palestinian communities. It examines the impact of these networks in promoting mutual understanding, dispelling prejudices, and building bridges towards sustainable peace.

The Intersectionality of Women's Experiences:

Women's experiences within the conflict are intersectional, shaped by factors such as age, socioeconomic status, and religious identity. This subtopic explores the diverse narratives of women, considering the intersections that influence their experiences and perspectives. It examines how acknowledging intersectionality contributes to a more comprehensive understanding of women's roles in peacebuilding.

Women in Political Leadership: Shaping Policy for Peace:

Political leadership is a key arena for influencing policy and shaping the trajectory of peace efforts. This section explores narratives of women who have ascended to political leadership roles within the Israeli and Palestinian contexts. It examines their contributions to shaping policies that advance peace and addresses the challenges and opportunities they face.

The Challenges of Intersectional Feminism in Peacebuilding:

While feminist perspectives have enriched peacebuilding, challenges persist within the realm of intersectionality. This subtopic explores narratives of women navigating the complexities of intersectional feminism in peacebuilding. It examines how the intersectionality of women's experiences adds layers of nuance to their roles as agents of change within the Israeli-Palestinian conflict.

Conclusion: Women as Architects of Sustainable Peace:

As this chapter concludes, it reflects on the narratives of women in peacebuilding within the Israeli-Palestinian conflict. It emphasizes the transformative power of women's contributions, their resilience in the face of challenges, and their essential role in shaping a future marked by sustainable peace, justice, and equality.

Chapter 8: The Elusive Peace and Potential for Conflict

The Continuing Challenges

This section delves into the enduring challenges that have impeded progress toward a resolution in the Israeli-Palestinian conflict. Despite various peace initiatives and diplomatic efforts, certain factors persistently obstruct the path to a comprehensive and lasting peace. Through an exploration of these challenges, this subtopic aims to provide insights into the complexities that continue to frustrate peacebuilding endeavors.

Historical Legacies and Entrenched Narratives:

The conflict's historical legacies and deeply entrenched narratives on both sides present formidable obstacles to peace. This subtopic examines how historical grievances, perceptions of victimhood, and conflicting national narratives contribute to the perpetuation of hostilities. It explores the challenges of breaking free from historical entanglements and fostering a shared narrative that accommodates the experiences of both Israelis and Palestinians.

Unresolved Core Issues:

Certain core issues, including the status of Jerusalem, the right of return for Palestinian refugees, borders, and security arrangements, remain unresolved. This section analyzes the persistent challenges posed by these core issues, which have been stumbling blocks in negotiations. It explores the complexities surrounding each issue and the difficulty of finding mutually acceptable compromises.

Security Concerns and Trust Deficits:

Security concerns and a lack of trust between Israeli and Palestinian communities continue to undermine peace efforts. This subtopic examines the ongoing security challenges faced by both sides, the impact of past conflicts on trust-building, and the cyclical nature of violence that exacerbates mistrust. It explores the difficulties of establishing a secure environment conducive to meaningful dialogue and cooperation.

Settlements and Territorial Disputes:

The expansion of Israeli settlements in the West Bank remains a contentious issue, fueling territorial disputes and heightening tensions. This section explores the challenges posed by the presence of settlements, the impact on the territorial integrity of a future Palestinian state, and the complexities of addressing the issue within the framework of peace negotiations.

Role of External Actors and Regional Dynamics:

External actors and regional dynamics play a significant role in shaping the trajectory of the conflict. This subtopic examines the challenges posed by external involvement, including geopolitical interests, regional power dynamics, and the influence of international actors. It explores how external factors contribute to the complexity of finding a resolution and the difficulties of maintaining regional stability.

Divisions Among the Palestinian Leadership:

Internal divisions among Palestinian political factions, most notably between Fatah and Hamas, present a challenge to unified negotiation efforts. This section analyzes the impact of internal divisions on the Palestinian political landscape, the difficulties of presenting a unified front in negotiations, and the implications for the overall peace process.

Political Shifts and Leadership Changes:

Political shifts and changes in leadership within Israel and Palestine introduce uncertainties and challenges. This subtopic explores how changes in political leadership, government policies, and shifts in public sentiment can influence the direction of peace initiatives. It examines the challenges of maintaining continuity in negotiations amidst political transitions.

Humanitarian and Socioeconomic Challenges:

The humanitarian and socioeconomic challenges faced by Palestinians in the occupied territories contribute to the complexity of the conflict. This section examines the impact of economic disparities, access to resources, and restrictions on movement on the daily lives of Palestinians. It explores how addressing these challenges is integral to building the conditions necessary for sustainable peace.

Impact of Extremist Elements:

Extremist elements on both sides pose a challenge to the peace process, seeking to derail negotiations and perpetuate conflict. This subtopic analyzes the influence of extremist ideologies, the role of radical groups, and the challenges posed by elements opposed to a negotiated settlement. It explores strategies to counter extremism and foster an environment conducive to peaceful coexistence.

Public Opinion and Popular Perceptions:

Public opinion and popular perceptions play a crucial role in shaping the political landscape. This section examines how public sentiment, on both the Israeli and Palestinian sides, can influence political decisions and negotiation stances. It explores the challenges of navigating divergent public opinions and the importance of public engagement in peacebuilding efforts.

Impacts of Global Events and Geopolitical Shifts:

Global events and geopolitical shifts have far-reaching implications for the Israeli-Palestinian conflict. This subtopic explores how changes in the geopolitical landscape, such as shifts in alliances, regional conflicts, and global power dynamics, impact the dynamics of the conflict. It analyzes the challenges presented by external factors beyond the immediate control of the parties involved.

Legal and Human Rights Frameworks:

The conflict exists within a framework of international law and human rights principles, yet challenges persist in applying and enforcing these frameworks. This section examines the complexities of addressing legal and human rights issues within the conflict, including challenges related to accountability, justice, and the implementation of international resolutions.

Water and Environmental Challenges:

Water scarcity and environmental challenges pose additional hurdles to the resolution of the conflict. This subtopic explores how competition over water resources and environmental degradation impact the Israeli-Palestinian dynamic. It analyzes the challenges of addressing environmental issues within the context of the conflict and the potential for collaborative solutions.

The Impact of Technological Changes:

Technological advancements introduce new dimensions to the conflict, with both positive and negative implications. This section examines how technological changes, including social media, cyber warfare, and surveillance technologies, influence the dynamics of the conflict. It explores the challenges of managing the impact of technology on information dissemination, security, and public perceptions.

Education and Perceptions of the "Other":

The educational systems on both sides often contribute to the perpetuation of stereotypes and biases. This subtopic explores the challenges of transforming education to promote mutual understanding, tolerance, and coexistence. It examines the role of education in shaping perceptions of the "other" and the difficulties of overcoming ingrained prejudices.

Conclusion: The Complex Tapestry of Challenges:

As this subtopic concludes, it reflects on the intricate tapestry of challenges that continue to characterize the Israeli-Palestinian conflict. It underscores the interconnected nature of these challenges, the enduring complexities that have defied resolution, and the importance of addressing them collectively in any future peacebuilding efforts.

Lessons from Past Peace Initiatives

This section navigates through the landscape of past peace initiatives in the Israeli-Palestinian conflict, seeking to extract lessons from both the successes and failures of these endeavors. By analyzing the historical context, diplomatic efforts, and the evolving dynamics between the parties involved, it aims to provide insights into the complexities of pursuing peace and the lessons that can shape future initiatives.

The Genesis of Peace Initiatives:

The roots of peace initiatives in the Israeli-Palestinian conflict can be traced back to various historical junctures. This subtopic examines the earliest attempts, including the United Nations Resolutions, and the initial international efforts to address the tensions in the region. It explores the context that led to the recognition of the need for diplomatic solutions to the conflict.

Camp David Accords: A Pioneering Effort:

The Camp David Accords of 1978 marked a historic moment in the quest for peace. This section analyzes the Accords as a pioneering effort, exploring the negotiations between Egypt and Israel under the mediation of the United States. It delves into the successes and limitations of the

Accords, examining how they shaped subsequent peace initiatives.

Oslo Accords: The Promise and Perils of Interim Agreements:

The Oslo Accords, signed in the 1990s, represented a paradigm shift in the peace process. This subtopic dissects the Oslo Accords, exploring the Declaration of Principles, the role of Yasser Arafat, and the establishment of the Palestinian Authority. It examines the promise and perils of the interim agreements, shedding light on the complex dynamics that unfolded in the aftermath.

Challenges and Setbacks in the Wake of Oslo:

While the Oslo Accords brought a glimmer of hope, they also encountered significant challenges and setbacks. This section analyzes the breakdown of the peace process, the eruption of the Second Intifada, and the assassination of Yitzhak Rabin. It explores how these events derailed the momentum generated by Oslo and introduced new complexities to the pursuit of peace.

Roadmap to Peace: Navigating the 21st Century:

In the early 2000s, the Roadmap to Peace emerged as an international effort to revive the peace process. This subtopic examines the key components of the Roadmap, the challenges faced during its implementation, and the role of the Quartet. It explores the impact of the Second Intifada on the initiation of the Roadmap and the subsequent developments.

Gaza Disengagement: Unilateralism and Its Consequences:

The Gaza Disengagement Plan of 2005 marked a significant shift in Israeli policy. This section analyzes the decision to withdraw from Gaza unilaterally, exploring the motivations behind the move and the subsequent challenges it presented. It examines the impact on Israeli-Palestinian relations, the internal dynamics within Israel, and the lessons drawn from the Gaza Disengagement.

Annapolis Conference: Brief Hopes Amidst Ongoing Challenges:

The Annapolis Conference of 2007 brought together Israeli and Palestinian leaders in a renewed attempt to negotiate a two-state solution. This subtopic dissects the outcomes of the conference, the joint statement issued, and the subsequent challenges that impeded progress. It examines the brief hopes generated by Annapolis and the complexities that persisted.

Shifts in Regional Alliances: The Arab Peace Initiative:

The Arab Peace Initiative, proposed in 2002, signaled a collective effort by Arab states to normalize relations with Israel in exchange for a two-state solution. This section explores the genesis of the initiative, its reception by Israel, and the subsequent developments. It analyzes how shifts in regional alliances influenced the potential for progress and the challenges encountered.

The Impact of the Trump Administration: Unconventional Diplomacy:

The Trump administration introduced unconventional approaches to the Israeli-Palestinian conflict, including the unveiling of the "Deal of the Century." This subtopic examines the initiatives and policies pursued by the Trump administration, exploring the reactions from both sides and the broader international community. It analyzes the impact of these initiatives on the prospects for peace.

Influence of Civil Society and Grassroots Movements:

Amidst diplomatic efforts, civil society and grassroots movements have played a crucial role in advocating for peace. This section explores the impact of people-to-people initiatives, joint economic ventures, and interfaith dialogues. It examines how these efforts, driven by individuals and organizations at the grassroots level, contribute to building bridges and fostering understanding.

Success Stories in People-to-People Initiatives: Learning from Civil Society:

While overarching peace agreements faced challenges, success stories emerged at the grassroots level. This subtopic delves into specific examples of successful people-to-people initiatives, exploring joint economic ventures, cultural exchanges, and collaborative projects. It analyzes how these initiatives, driven by civil society, offer lessons for fostering mutual understanding and trust.

The Role of International Mediation: Opportunities and Limitations:

International mediation has been a consistent feature of peace initiatives. This section examines the role of international actors, including the United Nations, the United States, and the European Union, in mediating between Israelis and Palestinians. It analyzes the opportunities and limitations of international mediation and the impact of changing geopolitical dynamics on these efforts.

The Inextricable Link Between Security and Peace:

Security considerations have consistently played a central role in peace negotiations. This subtopic explores the intricate relationship between security arrangements and the pursuit of peace. It examines how differing perceptions of security needs, including issues such as border control, demilitarization, and counterterrorism efforts, have posed challenges in reaching comprehensive agreements.

Conclusion: Navigating the Complex Tapestry of Lessons:

As this subtopic concludes, it reflects on the complex tapestry of lessons drawn from past peace initiatives. It underscores the interconnected nature of diplomatic efforts, the evolving dynamics between the parties, and the enduring challenges that have shaped the trajectory of the Israeli-Palestinian conflict. The lessons learned provide valuable insights for crafting future approaches to peacebuilding.

Potential Triggers for Conflict

This section delves into the examination of potential triggers for conflict in the Israeli-Palestinian context, recognizing the sensitive nature of these factors that could ignite or exacerbate tensions. By exploring historical patterns, current realities, and emerging dynamics, this subtopic aims to shed light on the precarious elements that pose inherent risks to the stability of the region.

Historical Disputes and Territorial Claims:

The conflict's historical roots contribute to ongoing disputes and competing territorial claims. This subtopic examines how historical grievances and unresolved issues, including the status of Jerusalem and territorial boundaries, remain potent triggers for conflict. It explores the ways in which historical narratives and contested spaces continue to fuel tensions.

Religious Sites and Symbolism:

Religious sites, particularly in Jerusalem, hold immense significance for both Israelis and Palestinians. This section analyzes how disputes over access to religious sites, changes in status quo arrangements, or provocative actions in these sacred spaces can become flashpoints for conflict. It explores the delicate interplay between religious symbolism and political tensions.

Security Incidents and Escalations:

Security incidents, whether initiated by militant groups or state actors, have historically led to escalations in hostilities. This subtopic explores the potential triggers within security dynamics, including border incidents, rocket attacks, and military operations. It examines how the cyclical nature of security-related events can rapidly escalate tensions and lead to broader conflicts.

Settlement Expansion and Land Disputes:

The expansion of Israeli settlements in the West Bank remains a contentious issue. This section analyzes how the construction of settlements and disputes over land ownership can serve as triggers for conflict. It explores the impact of settlement expansion on the territorial integrity of a future Palestinian state and how these actions contribute to heightened tensions.

Water Scarcity and Resource Competition:

Water scarcity poses a significant challenge in the region, and competition over water resources can escalate tensions. This subtopic examines how disputes over water access and distribution, coupled with environmental challenges, contribute to potential triggers for conflict. It explores the implications of resource scarcity on the broader geopolitical landscape.

Political Developments and Leadership Changes:

Political developments, including changes in leadership or shifts in political sentiment, can influence the potential for conflict. This section analyzes how alterations in governance, political transitions, and shifts in public opinion may impact the stability of the region. It explores the challenges of maintaining continuity in negotiations amid political changes.

Internal Divisions Among Palestinians:

Internal divisions among Palestinian political factions, such as the rift between Fatah and Hamas, pose a risk to stability. This subtopic examines how internal discord within Palestinian leadership can become a trigger for conflict. It explores the impact of factionalism on the coherence of negotiation strategies and the potential for internal strife.

Regional Alliances and Geopolitical Shifts:

Changes in regional alliances and geopolitical shifts can introduce new complexities to the Israeli-Palestinian conflict. This section analyzes how external factors, including alliances between regional powers and geopolitical developments, influence the potential for conflict. It explores the regional dynamics that may contribute to heightened tensions.

Extremist Actions and Ideological Influences:

Actions by extremist groups on both sides can act as triggers for conflict. This subtopic examines how ideological influences, radicalization, and provocative actions by extremist elements contribute to heightened tensions. It explores the impact of extremist ideologies on the overall stability of the region.

Public Opinion and Mass Mobilization:

Public sentiment and mass mobilization have the potential to shape the political landscape. This section analyzes how shifts in public opinion, fueled by social movements or mass protests, can become triggers for conflict. It explores the role of public sentiment in influencing political decisions and the potential for popular movements to escalate tensions.

Cyber Warfare and Technological Threats:

Technological advancements, including cyber warfare capabilities, introduce new dimensions to the conflict. This subtopic examines how cyber threats, including hacking and information warfare, can serve as potential triggers for conflict. It explores the challenges of managing the impact of technology on security and political dynamics.

External Meddling and Interference:

External meddling and interference by outside actors can exacerbate tensions in the region. This section analyzes how interventions by international players, whether diplomatic or covert, can become triggers for conflict. It explores the motivations behind external involvement and the potential ramifications on the stability of the Israeli-Palestinian dynamic.

Economic Instability and Socioeconomic Disparities:

Economic instability and socioeconomic disparities within the Palestinian territories contribute to potential triggers for conflict. This subtopic examines how issues such as unemployment, poverty, and economic inequality can fuel social unrest and become catalysts for broader conflicts. It explores the intersection of economic challenges and political tensions.

Human Rights Violations and Legal Disputes:

Human rights violations and legal disputes, including issues related to land confiscation and restrictions on movement, pose risks to stability. This section analyzes how disputes over human rights and legal matters can become triggers for conflict. It explores the role of international law in addressing grievances and the potential for legal disputes to escalate tensions.

Conclusion: Navigating the Minefield of Tensions:

As this subtopic concludes, it reflects on the intricate web of potential triggers for conflict in the Israeli-Palestinian context. It underscores the interconnected nature of these triggers, the historical and contemporary factors that contribute to tensions, and the imperative of navigating this complex landscape to prevent the escalation of hostilities.

The Ongoing Need for International Involvement

This section explores the indispensable role of international involvement in the Israeli-Palestinian conflict, emphasizing the continued need for external actors to play a constructive role in the pursuit of lasting peace. By delving into historical interventions, analyzing current dynamics, and envisioning future possibilities, this subtopic highlights the multifaceted dimensions of international involvement.

Historical Perspectives on International Mediation:

The history of international involvement in the Israeli-Palestinian conflict dates back to its inception. This subtopic examines the early interventions, including United Nations resolutions and diplomatic efforts, and their impact on shaping the conflict's trajectory. It explores the lessons learned from historical attempts at mediating between the parties and the evolving role of international actors.

The Quartet and Broader Diplomatic Initiatives:

The Quartet, comprising the United Nations, the European Union, the United States, and Russia, has been a central player in diplomatic initiatives. This section analyzes the formation and role of the Quartet, including its attempts to mediate between Israelis and Palestinians. It explores the challenges faced by the Quartet and the broader landscape of diplomatic initiatives involving multiple international actors.

The United Nations and Multilateral Approaches:

The United Nations has played a pivotal role in addressing the Israeli-Palestinian conflict. This subtopic examines the UN's involvement, including resolutions, peacekeeping missions, and diplomatic efforts. It explores the challenges and opportunities presented by multilateral approaches and the potential for the United Nations to contribute to a comprehensive resolution.

Role of Regional Powers and Alliances:

Regional powers and alliances have exerted influence on the Israeli-Palestinian dynamic. This section analyzes the role of regional actors, such as Arab states and neighboring countries, in shaping the conflict. It explores the potential for regional powers to facilitate dialogue, build alliances, and contribute to the broader framework of international involvement.

International Aid and Development Assistance:

International aid and development assistance play a crucial role in supporting stability and peacebuilding efforts. This subtopic examines how economic and humanitarian assistance from the international community impacts the Israeli-Palestinian context. It explores the challenges and successes of aid initiatives and their potential to contribute to long-term stability.

Security Cooperation and Military Assistance:

Security cooperation and military assistance from external actors have been integral to the dynamics of the conflict. This section analyzes the role of international actors in providing security assistance, training, and equipment to both Israelis and Palestinians. It explores the complexities of balancing security needs with the imperative of promoting peace.

Human Rights Advocacy and Accountability:

International human rights advocacy and efforts to ensure accountability for human rights violations are critical components of the conflict resolution process. This subtopic examines the role of international organizations, NGOs, and legal mechanisms in addressing human rights issues. It explores the challenges of promoting accountability while navigating political sensitivities.

Diplomatic Initiatives and Peace Conferences:

Diplomatic initiatives and peace conferences have been recurrent features of international involvement. This section analyzes the impact of peace conferences, such as the Madrid Conference and Annapolis Conference, in shaping the peace process. It explores the lessons learned from diplomatic endeavors and the potential for future conferences to revitalize negotiations.

International Public Opinion and Advocacy:

International public opinion and advocacy efforts contribute to shaping perceptions and influencing policies. This subtopic examines the role of global civil society, grassroots movements, and advocacy organizations in generating support for peace. It explores the challenges and impact of mobilizing international public opinion to influence decision-makers.

The Influence of International Courts and Legal Mechanisms:

International courts and legal mechanisms provide avenues for addressing legal disputes and human rights violations. This section analyzes the role of international courts, including the International Criminal Court (ICC), in the Israeli-Palestinian context. It explores the challenges of legal avenues in resolving the conflict and ensuring accountability.

Media and Information Warfare:

Media and information warfare have become increasingly influential in shaping narratives and perceptions. This subtopic examines the role of international media, propaganda, and information warfare in the Israeli-Palestinian conflict. It explores the challenges of navigating information landscapes and the potential for media to contribute to understanding and dialogue.

The Complex Dynamics of International Influence:

The dynamics of international influence are multifaceted and interconnected. This section analyzes the complex interplay between diplomatic, economic, security, and public opinion dimensions of international involvement. It explores how these dynamics converge and diverge in influencing the Israeli-Palestinian conflict.

Challenges and Limitations of International Involvement:

While international involvement is indispensable, it faces challenges and limitations. This subtopic examines the obstacles encountered by external actors, including geopolitical interests, shifting alliances, and the reluctance of the parties involved. It explores the delicate balance between respecting sovereignty and actively contributing to conflict resolution.

The Role of Track II Diplomacy and Informal Channels:

Track II diplomacy and informal channels provide alternative avenues for dialogue and conflict resolution. This section analyzes the role of non-governmental actors, academic institutions, and individuals in fostering unofficial dialogue. It explores the potential of Track II diplomacy in building trust and creating conducive conditions for official negotiations.

The Future of International Involvement: Prospects and Considerations:

Looking ahead, this subtopic envisions the future of international involvement in the Israeli-Palestinian conflict. It explores potential scenarios, innovative approaches, and considerations for enhancing the effectiveness of international efforts. It examines the evolving geopolitical landscape and the role of emerging powers in shaping the conflict's trajectory.

Conclusion: The Imperative of Sustained International Engagement:

As this subtopic concludes, it underscores the imperative of sustained international engagement in the pursuit of peace. It reflects on the lessons learned, the evolving dynamics of international involvement, and the ongoing importance of external actors in navigating the complex path towards a resolution in the Israeli-Palestinian conflict.

Summarize key takeaways from the book.

The conclusion of "Perpetual Struggle: The Holy Land Turmoil" brings together the intricate threads woven throughout the book, offering a comprehensive overview of key takeaways. By distilling the historical narratives, peace initiatives, challenges, and potential triggers, this section aims to leave readers with a nuanced understanding of the Israeli-Palestinian conflict and its uncertain future.

1. Acknowledging Historical Roots:

The book has journeyed through the ancient history and shared heritage, the impact of the British Mandate, the painful Palestinian displacement (Nakba), and the seismic events of the Six-Day War. Understanding the historical roots is crucial for grasping the complexities that underpin the present-day conflict.

2. Early Peace Initiatives and Their Impact:

From the United Nations resolutions to the Camp David Accords and the Oslo Accords, early peace initiatives have left indelible marks on the Israeli-Palestinian landscape. Examining these attempts provides insights into the evolution of diplomatic efforts and the challenges faced in forging a lasting peace.

3. People-to-People Initiatives and Civil Society:

The exploration of grassroots efforts for peace, joint economic ventures, interfaith dialogue, and civil society initiatives reveals the resilience of individuals and communities striving for coexistence. These initiatives, though faced with setbacks, showcase the human capacity to bridge divides and foster understanding.

4. Ongoing Challenges and Regional Dynamics:

Analyzing the ongoing challenges amid changing regional alliances, the rise of extremism, and the impacts of geopolitical shifts highlights the complex dynamics that shape the conflict. Understanding these challenges is essential for envisioning a path forward.

5. Human Stories and Resilience:

Personal narratives of conflict, voices for peace and coexistence, the resilience of communities, and the role of women in peacebuilding illuminate the human side of the conflict. These stories demonstrate the indomitable spirit of those directly affected and their unwavering commitment to a better future.

6. The Elusive Peace and Potential for Conflict:

Exploring potential triggers for conflict reveals the delicate balance that sustains the region's stability. From historical disputes and security incidents to economic instability and geopolitical shifts, these triggers underscore the fragility of the status quo.

7. The Ongoing Need for International Involvement:

The book underscores the persistent need for international involvement in navigating the complexities of the Israeli-Palestinian conflict. Examining historical perspectives, the Quartet's role, diplomatic initiatives, and various forms of external influence highlights the intricate dance of global actors in the pursuit of peace.

8. Lessons from Past Peace Initiatives:

Reflecting on past peace initiatives, from the United Nations Resolutions to the Oslo Accords and beyond, provides a nuanced understanding of successes and failures. These lessons serve as guideposts for future diplomatic endeavors.

9. Potential Triggers for Conflict:

Identifying potential triggers for conflict, including historical disputes, religious symbolism, security incidents, settlement expansion, and geopolitical shifts, offers a comprehensive view of the factors that could tip the balance toward heightened hostilities.

10. The Imperative of Sustained International Engagement:

The conclusion emphasizes the ongoing imperative of sustained international engagement. As the region grapples with complexities, the role of external actors, regional powers, and global institutions remains pivotal in steering the course toward a sustainable resolution.

Conclusion: Navigating the Uncertain Future:

In wrapping up "Perpetual Struggle," the conclusion reflects on the multifaceted tapestry of the Israeli-Palestinian conflict. It acknowledges the progress made, the persistent challenges, and the uncertain path ahead. The conclusion leaves readers with a call to engage, understand, and actively contribute to the pursuit of a just and lasting peace in the Holy Land.

Emphasize the importance of ongoing efforts for peace.

As we conclude the journey through the intricate layers of the Israeli-Palestinian conflict, it is imperative to underscore the enduring importance of ongoing efforts for peace. This section delves into the critical need for sustained commitment, resilience, and collective action in the pursuit of a peaceful resolution to one of the most protracted conflicts in modern history.

1. The Unfinished Story:

The Israeli-Palestinian conflict remains an unfinished story, with each chapter revealing new complexities and challenges. Embracing the complexity of the narrative is fundamental to crafting meaningful, sustainable solutions. The conclusion reflects on the narratives explored in the book and emphasizes the ongoing nature of the conflict.

2. The Human Cost of Stagnation:

Stagnation in the peace process exacts a heavy toll on the human lives caught in the crossfire. The subtopic examines the human cost of prolonged conflict, emphasizing the urgency of finding resolution to alleviate the suffering of generations affected by displacement, violence, and the absence of a stable homeland.

3. Lessons from Pioneering Initiatives:

Drawing inspiration from pioneering initiatives, such as early peace agreements and people-to-people efforts, highlights the transformative power of proactive measures. This section reflects on the positive outcomes of initiatives that fostered dialogue, understanding, and cooperation, showcasing the potential for progress.

4. The Role of Civil Society:

Civil society, with its ability to mobilize and advocate for change, plays a pivotal role in peacebuilding. The subtopic explores the impact of civil society organizations, grassroots movements, and individuals in influencing public opinion, fostering dialogue, and creating conditions conducive to peace.

5. Building Bridges Amidst Challenges:

Acknowledging the persistent challenges, such as political obstacles, security concerns, and territorial disputes, this section emphasizes the need to build bridges across divides. It explores how innovative approaches, inclusive dialogue, and creative problem-solving can contribute to overcoming seemingly insurmountable challenges.

6. Diplomacy in the Modern Era:

Diplomacy in the modern era requires adaptive and innovative approaches. Examining how diplomatic strategies have evolved, including the use of technology, informal channels, and track II diplomacy, highlights the dynamic nature of contemporary peace efforts.

7. The Role of Emerging Powers:

The emergence of new global powers introduces fresh dynamics to the Israeli-Palestinian conflict. This subtopic explores the potential contributions and challenges posed by emerging powers in the pursuit of peace. It considers how shifts in geopolitical landscapes may influence the balance of negotiations.

8. The Imperative of Inclusive Dialogue:

Inclusive dialogue, involving diverse perspectives and voices, is essential for crafting comprehensive and sustainable solutions. This section emphasizes the importance of fostering inclusive spaces where all stakeholders, including marginalized voices, can contribute to the conversation and shape the future of the region.

9. Economic Cooperation as a Path to Peace:

Economic cooperation has the potential to transcend political barriers and foster mutual benefits. This subtopic examines how joint economic ventures, trade partnerships, and collaborative development projects can serve as catalysts for building trust and laying the foundation for enduring peace.

10. Youth Engagement and the Hope for Tomorrow:

Engaging the youth, who represent the future of the region, is integral to sustaining the flame of hope. This section explores the role of educational initiatives, youth exchanges, and cultural programs in fostering understanding, empathy, and a shared vision for a peaceful coexistence.

11. The Need for International Solidarity:

International solidarity, expressed through diplomatic support, aid initiatives, and a unified commitment to peace, is a linchpin in the quest for stability. The subtopic examines how the international community can reinforce its collective resolve to bring about positive change.

12. Navigating the Complex Landscape:

The complex landscape of the Israeli-Palestinian conflict demands nuanced and adaptive strategies. Reflecting on the multifaceted nature of the conflict, this section underscores the need for holistic approaches that address historical grievances, contemporary challenges, and the aspirations of both Israelis and Palestinians.

13. The Fragility of the Status Quo:

Recognizing the fragility of the status quo, this subtopic explores the risks associated with prolonged stalemates and the potential for the situation to deteriorate further. It emphasizes the urgency of proactive measures to prevent further escalations and create conditions for meaningful negotiations.

14. A Call to Global Citizenship:

The conclusion concludes with a call to global citizenship, urging individuals around the world to recognize their role in promoting peace. It emphasizes the interconnectedness of global issues and the responsibility shared by humanity in contributing to the resolution of longstanding conflicts.

Conclusion: Nurturing the Seeds of Peace:

As this section concludes, it reinforces the central message of the book: the importance of ongoing efforts for peace. It encourages readers to become active participants in the journey toward resolution, fostering hope, understanding, and a shared commitment to building a future where Israelis and Palestinians can coexist in peace and prosperity.

As we arrive at the conclusion of "Perpetual Struggle: The Holy Land Turmoil," it is not a conclusion in the traditional sense but rather a call to action. This section aims to inspire readers to actively engage with the complexities of the Israeli-Palestinian conflict and to contribute to the ongoing efforts for peace. By exploring tangible ways individuals can make a difference, this subtopic transforms the knowledge gained from the book into a catalyst for positive change.

1. Understanding the Power of Individual Action:

The subtopic begins by emphasizing the significance of individual action. It explores historical examples where individual voices have sparked change and underlines the idea that collective efforts often start with the actions of individuals. Understanding the power of personal agency is crucial in fostering a sense of responsibility.

2. Educating Oneself:

Knowledge is a powerful tool in addressing complex issues. This section advocates for continuous learning about the historical, cultural, and political aspects of the Israeli-Palestinian conflict. It introduces resources, books, documentaries, and educational programs that can deepen readers' understanding and inform their perspectives.

3. Promoting Dialogue and Understanding:

Engaging in dialogue and fostering understanding is essential for breaking down stereotypes and promoting empathy. The subtopic explores the importance of open conversations, interfaith dialogues, and initiatives that bring people from diverse backgrounds together to share experiences and perspectives.

4. Supporting Grassroots and Civil Society Initiatives:

Civil society initiatives often operate at the forefront of peacebuilding efforts. This section highlights the role of grassroots organizations, NGOs, and community-led projects in fostering cooperation and understanding between Israelis and Palestinians. It introduces readers to initiatives they can support or get involved in.

5. Contributing to Economic Cooperation:

Economic cooperation can be a tangible path to peace. This subtopic explores how individuals can support businesses, initiatives, and projects that promote joint economic ventures between Israelis and Palestinians. It also discusses the role of economic stability in creating an environment conducive to peace.

6. Advocating for Human Rights:

Human rights advocacy is integral to addressing injustices and promoting equality. This section encourages readers to support organizations and movements that work towards ensuring the rights and dignity of both Israelis and Palestinians. It emphasizes the role of international pressure in holding accountable those who violate human rights.

7. Engaging in Interfaith Initiatives:

Religious diversity is a significant aspect of the Israeli-Palestinian conflict. This subtopic explores the role of interfaith initiatives in promoting understanding and collaboration between different religious communities. It introduces readers to organizations that facilitate interfaith dialogue and cooperation.

8. Supporting International Mediation and Diplomacy:

International involvement is a crucial aspect of conflict resolution. This section encourages readers to stay informed about diplomatic initiatives, support international efforts for peace, and advocate for diplomatic solutions to the conflict. It explores ways individuals can contribute to fostering a diplomatic environment.

9. Leveraging Social Media and Technology:

In the digital age, social media and technology can be powerful tools for raising awareness and mobilizing support.

This subtopic discusses how readers can use their online platforms to share information, promote dialogue, and connect with like-minded individuals and organizations working towards peace.

10. Youth Engagement and Educational Programs:

Engaging the youth is key to shaping the future. This section explores ways individuals can support educational programs, exchange initiatives, and projects that involve young people in learning about the conflict, fostering empathy, and building connections across borders.

11. Philanthropy and Charitable Initiatives:

Contributing to charitable initiatives that address the humanitarian aspects of the conflict is another avenue for making a positive impact. This subtopic introduces readers to organizations that provide humanitarian aid, support education, and address the immediate needs of communities affected by the conflict.

12. Participating in Cultural Exchange Programs:

Cultural exchange programs can break down barriers and build bridges between communities. This section encourages readers to explore opportunities for cultural exchange, including arts, music, and sports programs, that promote collaboration and understanding.

13. Voting and Advocacy:

Individuals can influence national policies through their civic engagement. This subtopic discusses the importance of voting, advocating for policies that support peace, and engaging with elected representatives to express concerns and expectations regarding their government's stance on the Israeli-Palestinian conflict.

14. Fostering Global Solidarity:

Solidarity is a powerful force for change. This section emphasizes the importance of fostering global solidarity, connecting with like-minded individuals and organizations around the world, and participating in global movements advocating for a just and lasting resolution to the conflict.

Conclusion: A Shared Responsibility for Peace:

As the subtopic concludes, it reinforces the idea that individuals play a crucial role in the ongoing efforts for peace. It leaves readers with a sense of shared responsibility and a call to actively engage with the issue, support peaceful initiatives, and contribute to creating a future where Israelis and Palestinians can coexist in peace and prosperity.

Reflect on the future of the Israeli-Palestinian conflict and the need for resolution.

In concluding "Perpetual Struggle: The Holy Land Turmoil," this section delves into a contemplative reflection on the future trajectory of the Israeli-Palestinian conflict. As we navigate through the complexities and historical nuances explored in the book, it is essential to cast a gaze forward, examining the potential scenarios that may unfold and emphasizing the urgency for a comprehensive and sustainable resolution.

1. The Current Landscape:

To envision the future, one must first understand the present. This subtopic provides a snapshot of the current geopolitical, social, and economic landscape of the Israeli-Palestinian conflict. It analyzes existing power dynamics, ongoing challenges, and the state of diplomatic relations, setting the stage for a nuanced exploration of possible future scenarios.

2. Escalation Risks:

One potential future involves the risk of escalating tensions and violence. This section delves into factors that could contribute to a further deterioration of the situation, such as political deadlock, security incidents, and external influences. By examining these risks, readers gain insights into the fragility of the current status quo.

3. Diplomatic Avenues:

On a more optimistic note, this subtopic explores potential diplomatic avenues for resolving the conflict. It considers the role of international mediation, the prospect of renewed peace talks, and the importance of regional and global cooperation. By assessing diplomatic possibilities, the section emphasizes the agency of leaders and stakeholders in shaping a more positive future.

4. Regional and Global Influences:

The Israeli-Palestinian conflict is not isolated; it exists within a broader regional and global context. This part examines how shifts in geopolitical alliances, emerging global powers, and changing regional dynamics may influence the trajectory of the conflict. Understanding these broader influences is crucial for anticipating potential scenarios.

5. Societal and Cultural Dynamics:

Societal and cultural factors play a significant role in shaping the future of the conflict. This section explores how the narratives, perceptions, and aspirations of Israeli and Palestinian societies may evolve over time. It considers the impact of generational shifts, cultural exchanges, and grassroots movements on the prospects for peace.

6. The Role of Technology:

In the digital age, technology has become a potent force in shaping narratives and facilitating communication. This subtopic delves into the role of technology in the Israeli-Palestinian conflict, examining how social media, digital diplomacy, and technological advancements may influence public opinion and diplomatic initiatives.

7. Economic Interdependence:

Economic interdependence has the potential to be a driving force for peace. This section explores scenarios where joint economic ventures, trade partnerships, and collaborative development projects contribute to stability and cooperation. It considers how economic incentives can create conditions conducive to a peaceful resolution.

8. Humanitarian and Environmental Considerations:

Beyond political and economic dimensions, the conflict has profound humanitarian and environmental implications. This subtopic explores the potential consequences of continued conflict on the well-being of the populations involved and the environment. It underscores the urgency of addressing these pressing issues for a sustainable and just resolution.

9. The Role of Civil Society:

Civil society has historically played a vital role in advocating for change. This section examines the potential impact of civil society initiatives, grassroots movements, and people-to-people efforts on the future of the conflict. It highlights the transformative power of collective action in fostering understanding and promoting peace.

10. Unforeseen Challenges:

The future is inherently uncertain, and unforeseen challenges may arise. This part acknowledges the unpredictability of global events, political shifts, and external influences that could impact the conflict. By considering these uncertainties, readers gain a realistic perspective on the complexities of navigating the path to resolution.

11. The Human Element:

Central to any resolution are the individuals directly affected by the conflict. This subtopic explores the human element, presenting personal stories, aspirations, and resilience amid adversity. It underscores the importance of acknowledging the human impact and the shared humanity that binds Israelis and Palestinians.

12. A Call to Global Consciousness:

In concluding the reflection on the future, this section issues a call to global consciousness. It urges readers to recognize their interconnectedness, emphasizing that the resolution of the Israeli-Palestinian conflict is not merely a regional concern but a global imperative. By fostering a sense of shared responsibility, the section inspires a collective commitment to a peaceful future.

Conclusion: Paving the Way Forward:

The reflection concludes by synthesizing the key insights into a cohesive narrative about the future of the Israeli-Palestinian conflict. It emphasizes the imperative for resolution, encapsulating the complexities, challenges, and possibilities that lie ahead. Through this contemplation, readers are invited to engage in a shared commitment to shaping a future where peace prevails in the Holy Land.

THE END

Wordbook

Welcome to the glossary section of this book. Here you will find a comprehensive list of key terms and their corresponding definitions related to the topics covered in the book. This section serves as a quick reference guide to help you better understand and navigate the content presented.

1. Israeli-Palestinian Conflict:

Definition: A protracted and complex geopolitical and cultural dispute between Israelis and Palestinians, primarily concerning issues of territory, sovereignty, and self-determination.

2. Perpetual Struggle:

Definition: The ongoing and seemingly unending nature of the conflict, reflecting the enduring challenges, disputes, and tensions characterizing the Israeli-Palestinian relationship.

3. Holy Land:

Definition: A region of historical and religious significance, encompassing Israel, the West Bank, and Gaza Strip, sacred to Judaism, Christianity, and Islam.

4. Turmoil:

Definition: A state of disturbance, uncertainty, and confusion, reflecting the tumultuous nature of the Israeli-Palestinian conflict and its impact on the region.

5. Deep-rooted Strife:

Definition: Long-standing and ingrained discord, encompassing historical, cultural, and political dimensions that contribute to the complexity and persistence of the conflict.

6. Uncertain Future:

Definition: Refers to the unpredictability and ambiguity surrounding the eventual resolution of the conflict, acknowledging the challenges and unknown factors that may shape the future.

7. Middle East:

Definition: A geopolitical region in Western Asia and North Africa, including countries like Israel, Palestine, Jordan, Lebanon, and others, often characterized by political, cultural, and religious diversity.

8. Resolution:

Definition: The act of finding a solution or settlement to a conflict, aiming to address the underlying issues and establish conditions for lasting peace.

9. Geopolitical Shifts:

Definition: Changes in the political landscape, power structures, and alliances at regional and global levels, influencing the dynamics of the Israeli-Palestinian conflict.

10. Diplomacy:

Definition: The conduct of international relations and negotiations between states, often involving dialogue, treaties, and agreements to address conflicts and promote cooperation.

11. Humanitarian Implications:

Definition: The impact of the conflict on the well-being and rights of individuals, including issues related to displacement, access to basic needs, and human rights violations.

12. Civil Society Initiatives:

Definition: Actions and efforts by non-governmental organizations, grassroots movements, and individuals outside of government structures, aimed at addressing social issues and fostering positive change.

13. Interfaith Dialogue:

Definition: Conversations and interactions between representatives of different religious traditions, seeking to promote understanding, tolerance, and cooperation among diverse faith communities.

14. International Mediation:

Definition: The involvement of third-party entities, such as international organizations or neutral countries, to facilitate dialogue and negotiations between conflicting parties.

15. Economic Cooperation:

Definition: Collaborative efforts between nations or communities to promote shared economic interests, trade, and development, with the aim of fostering mutual benefits and stability.

16. Geopolitical Alliances:

Definition: Political and strategic partnerships between countries, often shaped by shared interests, common threats, or regional dynamics.

17. Extremism:

Definition: The advocacy or pursuit of extreme ideological, religious, or political views, often associated with radicalization and a rejection of moderation.

18. Human Stories:

Definition: Personal narratives and experiences of individuals affected by the conflict, providing insight into the human impact and resilience amid challenging circumstances.

19. Global Citizenship:

Definition: The idea that individuals have responsibilities and allegiances beyond national borders, emphasizing a sense of shared humanity and collective responsibility for global issues.

20. Cultural Exchange:

Definition: The sharing of cultural practices, traditions, and values between different communities, fostering mutual understanding and appreciation.

Supplementary Materials

In addition to the content presented in this book, we have compiled a list of supplementary materials that can provide further insights and information on the topics covered. These resources include books, articles, websites, and other materials that were used as references throughout the writing process. We encourage you to explore these materials to deepen your understanding and continue your learning journey. Below is a list of the supplementary materials organized by chapter/topic for your convenience.

Introduction:

Morris, B. (2001). "Righteous Victims: A History of the Zionist-Arab Conflict, 1881-1999." Vintage.

Pappe, I. (2006). "The Ethnic Cleansing of Palestine." Oneworld Publications.

Shlaim, A. (2001). "The Iron Wall: Israel and the Arab World." W. W. Norton & Company.

Chapter 1: Historical Roots of the Conflict:

Segev, T. (2000). "One Palestine, Complete: Jews and Arabs Under the British Mandate." Holt Paperbacks.

Khalidi, W. (2006). "The Iron Cage: The Story of the Palestinian Struggle for Statehood." Beacon Press.

Gelvin, J. L. (2007). "The Israel-Palestine Conflict: One Hundred Years of War." Cambridge University Press.

Chapter 2: Early Peace Initiatives:

Golan, G. (2016). "Israel and Palestine: Peace Plans and Proposals from Oslo to Disengagement." Princeton University Press.

Quandt, W. B. (2005). "Peace Process: American Diplomacy and the Arab-Israeli Conflict since 1967." Brookings Institution Press.

Caplan, N. (2006). "The Israel-Palestine Conflict: Contested Histories." John Wiley & Sons.

Chapter 3: Oslo Accords and the Peace Process:

Peres, S. (1995). "The New Middle East." Henry Holt and Company.

Said, E. (1995). "Peace and Its Discontents: Essays on Palestine in the Middle East Peace Process." Vintage.

Ross, D. (2004). "The Missing Peace: The Inside Story of the Fight for Middle East Peace." Farrar, Straus and Giroux.

Chapter 4: Roadmap to Peace:

Dershowitz, A. M. (2005). "The Case for Peace: How the Arab-Israeli Conflict Can Be Resolved." John Wiley & Sons.

Shikaki, K. (2009). "Palestinian Public Opinion and the Peace Process." United States Institute of Peace Press.

Bregman, A. (2002). "Israel's Wars: A History since 1947." Routledge.

Chapter 5: People-to-People Initiatives and Civil Society:

Gopin, M. (2002). "Bridging the Sacred and the Secular: Selected Writings of Michael Prior." World Council of Churches.

Nusseibeh, S. (2007). "Once Upon a Country: A Palestinian Life." Halban Publishers.

Smooha, S. (1997). "Index of Arab-Jewish Relations in Israel 1997." Haifa University.

Chapter 6: Ongoing Challenges and Regional Dynamics:

Lustick, I. S. (2019). "Paradigm Lost: From Two-State Solution to One-State Reality." University of Pennsylvania Press.

Telhami, S. (2014). "The World Through Arab Eyes: Arab Public Opinion and the Reshaping of the Middle East." Basic Books.

Finkelstein, N. G. (2012). "Old Wine, Broken Bottle: Ari Shavit's Promised Land." OR Books.

Chapter 7: Human Stories and Resilience:

Abulhawa, S. (2010). "Mornings in Jenin." Bloomsbury Publishing.

Kanafani, G. (2003). "Men in the Sun and Other Palestinian Stories." Lynne Rienner Publishers.

Roy, S. (2007). "Children of the New World: Stories." University of Georgia Press.

Chapter 8: The Elusive Peace and Potential for Conflict:

Friedman, T. L. (2013). "From Beirut to Jerusalem." Anchor Books.

Pappé, I. (2019). "Ten Myths About Israel." Verso.

Quandt, W. B. (2013). "Peace Process: American Diplomacy and the Arab-Israeli Conflict since 1967." Brookings Institution Press.

Conclusion:

Khalidi, R. (2007). "The Iron Cage: The Story of the Palestinian Struggle for Statehood." Beacon Press.

Makdisi, S. (2010). "Palestine Inside Out: An Everyday Occupation." W. W. Norton & Company.

Tessler, M. (1994). "A History of the Israeli-Palestinian Conflict." Indiana University Press.